PRÁCTICA PARA EXÁMENES DE CIUDADANÍA

Carlos F. Paz

ARCO
New York

Second Edition

ARCO

Simon & Schuster, Inc.
Gulf+Western Building
One Gulf+Western Plaza
New York, NY 10023

DISTRIBUTED BY PRENTICE HALL TRADE

Manufactured in the United States of America

2 3 4 5 6 7 8 9 10

Library of Congress Cataloging-in-Publication Data

Paz, Carlos F.
Práctica para exámenes de ciudadania
Carlos F. Paz.
p. cm.
ISBN 0-13-705083-1 : $5.95 (est.)
1. Emigration and immigration law—United States—Popular works.
2. Alien labor—United States—Popular works. 3. Aliens, Illegal-
-United States—Popular works. 4. Citizenship—United States-
-Popular works. I. Title.
KF4800.Z9P39 1988
342.73′082—dc19 88-15088
[347.30282] CIP

Contenido

Preface

What this book is all about:

In brief and simple language this book presents the requirements for naturalization, a short history of the United States and its government, and examples of the kinds of questions you will be asked in the written and oral examinations. The information provided here is not meant to take the place of the United States Immigration and Naturalization Service pamphlets, but simply to give additional help to the men and women who wish to become United States citizens.

This book includes the basic facts, laws, and regulations you need to know to become a citizen, plus over 200 sample questions of the sort used by examiners.

Carlos F. Paz

Prólogo

Acerca de lo que se trata en este libro:

En lenguaje sencillo y conciso, este libro le explica los requisitos que usted debe llenar para poder obtener la Naturalización. Aquí le ofrecemos una breve historia de los Estados Unidos y de su sistema de gobierno, y le proporcionamos ejemplos de los tipos de preguntas que usted puede esperar cuando tome las pruebas orales y escritas. La información que le brindamos no tiene como propósito reemplazar los folletos del Servicio de Inmigración y Naturalización, sino sencillamente ofrecerle una ayuda adicional a los hombres y mujeres que desean adquirir la ciudadanía de los Estados Unidos.

Este libro contiene las leyes, reglas y datos principales que usted debe conocer para convertirse en ciudadano americano, y más de 200 ejemplos del tipo de preguntas que hacen los examinadores.

Carlos F. Paz

Resumen de la Ley de Reforma y Control de Inmigración de 1986

La Ley de Reforma y Control de Inmigración de 1986 fue firmada por el presidente Reagan el 6 de noviembre de 1986. Los principales elementos doe la nueva ley son las sanciones contra los empleadores que a sabiendas emplean a extranjeros indocumentados y la legalización de algunos extranjeros indocumentados que llenan ciertos requisitos.

LEGALIZACIÓN DE EXTRANJEROS INDOCUMENTADOS

Gran parte de la nueva ley do inmigración es la legalización de extranjeros indocumentados que llenan ciertos requisitos especificos. Para ser elegible para amnistía, la persona extranjera tiene que comprobar residencia ilegal continua en los Estados Unidos desde antes del 1º de enero de 1982. Sin embargo, los extranjeros condenados por un delito mayor o tres delitos menores pierden la oportunidad de legalización. A los extranjeros legalizados se les da residencia temporal por un período de dieciocho meses, después del cual tienen un año para solicitar residencia permanente. *Para hacerse residente permanente, la persona tiene que demostrar conocimientos minimos del inglés y de la historia y el gobierno de los Estados Unidos.* A los cinco años de ser residente permanente, el extranjero puede solicitar la ciudadanía. Durante ese período de cinco años, el extranjero no es elegible para recibir bienestar social, estampillas o sellos de alimentos y muchos otros beneficios federales.

El programa de amnistía, de un año de duración, empizó el 5 de mayo de 1987. como parte del proceso de solicitud, el extranjero tiene que proporcionar prueba ce haber estado en los Estados Unidos por los cinco años que especifica la ley, con la excepción de "ausencias breves, casuales o inocentes". Tales ausencias pueden ser hasta de 45 días durante un período o un total de 180 días durante el período de cinco años.

La duración de estas ausencias permitidas es menor si la persona indocumentada ha salido del país después de que se pasaron los reglamentos, pro ejemplo, el 1º de mayo de 1986. En tal caso, se le permiten "ausencias breves, casuales o inocentes", definidas como una ausencia de hasta 30 días en un período o un total de hasta 90 días. El sistema actual del INS exige que el extranjero obtenga aprobación para salir de los Estados Unidos después del 1º de mayo de 1987 ó si no pierde la oportunidad de legalización.

Para comprobar que que ha vivido aquí cinco años, la persona que solicita amnistía puede mostrar distintos documentos, entre ellos, comprobantes de pago, formularios de impuestos o de deducciones, recibos de alquiler, cuentas de electricidad, agua o gas, o estado do cuenta bancaria. El gobierno prefiere "documentos relacionados con el trabajo" y puede exigir "corroboración independiente" de cualquier documento. Al solicitante también se le permite presentar "atestiguación escrita de testigos creíbles" como evidencia adicional a su favor.

Para facilitar el proceso de registro y legalización, el INS ha designado iglesias y grupos de la comunidad para proporcionar consejería a los inducumentados y ayudar en la preparación de las solicitudes. Estas agencias revisan las solicitudes de los indocumentados e informan a los solicitantes cuando no son elegibles para amnistía.

SANCIONES PARA EMPLEADORES

A pesar de que en el pasado ha sido ilegal que los extranjeros indocumentados trabajen en los Estados Unidos, no ha sido sino hasta ahora que la ley prohibe a los empleadores contratar a los indocumentados. Con la aprobación de esta nueva ley de inmigración, los empleadores están ahora sujetos a pena legal y en última instancia, encarcelamiento, si "a sabiendas" contratan, reclutan o refieren por comisión a cualquier extranjero sin autorización. Igualmente, es un delito el que los empleadores continúen empleando a cualquier extranjero contratado después del 6 de noviembre do 1986, a sabiendas de que esa persona no tiene autorización de trabajo. (Se hace una excepción en el caso de trabajadores agrícolas hasta el 30 de noviembre de 1988.)

De acuerdo con la tabla de penas, después de una amonestación, al empleador se le impone multa de entre $250 y $2,000 por cada indocumentado cuando se trata de la primera infracción; una multa de entre $2,000 y $5,000 por la segunda infracción; y una multa de entre $3,000 y $10,000 por la tercer infracción. Cuando se hace "práctica" de delitos particularmente flagrantes, el empleador puede enfrentarse a penas criminales de hasta $3,000 y seis meses de cárcel.

Para evitar tales penas, el empleado debe cumplir ciertos procedimientos específicos de verificación. El presunto empleador debe exigir al solicitante de empleo que presente documentación que le identifiquen al igual que la autorización para trabajar en los Estados Unidos. Documentos do identidad pueden ser la licencia de conducir, pasaporte u otro documento oficial con fotografía. Documentos de "autorización de trabajo" pueden ser la tarjeta de seguro social, certificado de nacimiento de los Estados Unidos o cualquier otro documento que pruebe específicamente que hay autorización para trabajar. Documentos que llenan ambos requisitos para el presunto empleador pueden ser pasaporte de Estados Unidos, certificado de nacionalidad de Estados Unidos, certificado de naturalización, pasaporte extranjero válido con autorización de trabajo, o "tarjeta verde" (la tarjeta oficial de registro de un extranjero). Hasta el 1º de septiembre de 1987, los empleadores podían contratar a extanjeros indocumentados con planes de solicitar amnistía y simplemente escribir en el Formulario I-9 que la persona indocumentada ha dicho que es elegible para amnistía y va a hacer la solicitud.

DISCRIMINACIÓN

Los empleadores que piensan evitar posibles problemas si contratan a extranjeros y solamente contratan a ciudadanos de Estados Unidos también violan las provisiones antidiscriminatorias de la nueva ley de inmmigración. No es delito el seleccionar a un ciudadano de Estados Undios y no a un extranjero si ambos están igualmente capacitados, Sin embargo, es ilegal que el empleador discrimine a un residente legal con base en su situación de ciudadanía o país de origen.

PROVISIONES AGRÍCOLAS

Las condiciones de amnistía en la industria agrícola difieren de las de otras industrias. Para ser elegible para residencia temporal, los trabajadores agrícolas tienen que haber trabajado en la agricultura dentro de los Estados Unidos solamente 90 días entre mayo de 1985 y mayo de 1986. Hay diferentes períodos para hacerse residentes permanentes, de acuerdo con cuántas temporadas hayan trabajado las personas en los Estados Unidos.

La nueva ley también tiene provisiones para reponer la fuerza laboral de temporada permitiendo que nuevos trabajadores entren al país como residentes temporales si hay escasez de trabajadores agrícolas. Otra diferencia se la nueva ley entre la agricultura y otras industrias es que la sanciones no se empiezan a aplicar a los empleadores de trabajadores agrícolas de temporada sino hasta el 1º de diciembre de 1988.

Datos Sobre la Ley de Inmigración

Legalización

- La ley de Reforma y Control de Inmigración (IRCA en inglés) de 1986 fue firmada por el presidente Reagan el 6 de noviembre de 1986.
- A partir del 5 de mayo de 1987, los extranjeros que han residido de manera continua e ilegal en los Estados Unidos desde antes del 1º de enero de 1982, podrán hacer solicitud para legalizar su situación. A toda persona cuya solicitud se apruebe se le concederá residencia legal temporalmente y se le dará autorización para trabajar.
- El período para hacer solicitud tendrá duración de doce meses solamente, hasta el 4 de mayo de 1988.
- Alrededor de 100 oficinas de legalización se abrirán el 5 de mayo de por todo el país. Se esperan hasta 16,000 solicitudes diarias.
- A los dieciocho meses de haber recibido residencia legal temporal, se espera que los extranjeros hagan solicitud de residencia legal permanente—el primer paso para la ciudadanía de Estados Unidos.

Consejos del INS para los empleadores

- Se debe estar alerta a la información de acatamiento proveniente del gobierno durante el período de información.

- Manifestar la intención de contratar solamente a trabajadores legales.

- Informar a todos los empleados nuevos que cuando se reciban nuevas guías se les informará sobre las responsabilidades que les asigna la ley.

- No despedir o negarse a emplear a ninguna persona por tener aspecto extranjero ni por el idioma.

- A los empleadores no se les castigará por personas contratadas antes del 6 de noviembre de 1986.

Fechas importantes y períodos para recordar

6 de noviembre de 1986	Fecha en que el presidente Reagan firmó la Ley de Reforma y Control de Inmigración. En esta fecha se convirtió en delito el que los empleadores contrataran a sabiendas a extranjeros indocumentados.
1º de diciembre de 1986 a 31 de mayo de 1987	Este es el período de educación del público. Durante este períod no se dará amonestación alguna a los empleadores por transgresión de la ley.

1º de julio de 1987 a 31 de mayo de 1987	A los empleadores que se les encuentre culpables de contratar, reclutar o referir a extranjeros indocumentados se les dará una amonestación por la primera transgresión. Por las transgresiones siguientes, el empleado se enfrentará a penas civiles y criminales.
1º de junio de 1988	A partir de esta fecha, los empleadores que contraten, recluten o refieran para empleo a extranjeros indocumentados, se enfrentarán a penas civiles por la primera transgresión (excepto cuando se trata de trabajadores agrícolas de temporada).
1º de diciembre de 1988	Esta es la primera fecha en que se pueden imponer sanciones civiles a los empleadores de trabajadores agrígolas de temporada.

Datos Sobre la Legalización

Quien Califica

Los extranjeros indocumentados que han vivido en los Estados Unidos desde antes de enero de 1982 son elegibles para legalización si:

- no han salido de los Estados Unidos desde el 1º de enero de 1982, excepto durante ausencias breves y casuales. ("Breves" y "casuales" se definen como ausencias de los Estados Unidos no mayores de 45 días en una sola salida y de no más do un total de 180 días en cualquier número de salidas.)
- no han sido condenados de un delito mayor o tres o más delitos menores y son aceptables en otros respectos.

Pasos para la Legalización

- Obtener las solicitudes, incluso los formularios para examen médico obligatorio, en una oficina de legalización, entidades debidamente designadas, proveedores directos de servicio, o abogados. Las siguientes cuotas deben acompañar la solicitud al momento de presentarla:

adultos	$185
niños	$ 50
familia	$420

Las cuotas se pueden pagar con cheque de caja, giro bancario, o giro postal. Los giros se deben pagar a favor del U.S. Immigration and Naturalization Service.

- Llenar el formulario de solicitud. Pueden proporcionar ayuda para llenarlo las entidades debidamente designadas, proveedores directos de servicio, o abogados. Estas personas pueden cobrar por sus servicios.

- Lo siguiente se debe presentar con la solicitud de cada beneficiario.

1. Dos fotos a color tipo pasaporte, 2 pulgadas por 2 pulgadas, que se pueden obtener donde toman fotos para pasaportes o en entidades debidamente designadas. Una hoja de especificaciones se incluirá con la solicitud.
2. Dos juegos de huellas digitales, las cuales se pueden obtener de agencias voluntarias y departamentos de la policía. En algunas oficinas de legalización puede haber servicio de fotos y de huellas digitales.
3. Un formulario de examen médico llenada por un médico aprobado. Una lista de médicos aprobados se incluirá con la solicitud.
4. Requisitos de documentos originales para comprobar identidad y residencia.

   A. Prueba de identidad (por lo menos uno de los siguientes)
   pasaporte
   certificado de nacimiento
   tarjeta o cédula de identidad del país de origen
   licencia de conducir del estado
   certificados de bautismo/certificado de matrimonio
   atestiguaciones escritas

   B. Prueba de residencia (cualesquiera dos de los siguientes)

   documentos de empleos anteriores, como:

formularios de impuesto
cartas de empleadores
cartas de bancos si trabaja por cuenta propia
recibos de electricidad, agua, o gas
recibos de alquiler
expedientes escolares

- Cuando todos los documentos estén eompletos, deben presentarse a una oficina se legalización. Algunas de ellas exigen que se presente en persona. No se necesita cita, El momento de hacerlo y las horas de oficina varían de una oficina a otra. Las solicitudes se deben llenar a más tardar el 4 de mayo de 1988.
- Cuando se presente la solicitud, el solicitante recibirá un documento de identificación con autorización para trabajar y se fijará fecha para una entrevista.
- Si se rechaza una solicitud, la información se mantendrá en la más estricta confidencia excepto en casos de fraude documentos falsificados o adulterados).

Oficinas de Inmigración y Legalización

Servicio de Naturalización y de Inmigración de los Estados Unidos

U.S. Immigration Naturalization Service

Directory of Legalization Offices

ALASKA

Michael Building
620 E. 10th Avenue
Suite 102
Anchorage, AK 99510

ARIZONA

3420 So. 7th Street
Phoenix, AZ 85040

4600 So. Park Avenue, Suite #5
Tuscon, AZ 85714

281 West Maley
Willcox, AZ 85643

1325 West 16th Street
Yuma, AZ 85364

CALIFORNIA

1011 17th Street
Bakersfield, CA 93301

9858 Artesia Boulevard
Bellflower, CA 90706

7342 Orangethorpe Avenue
Buena Park, CA 90621

1627 West Main Street
El Centro, CA 92243

9660 Flair Drive
El Monte, CA 91731

463 North Midway Drive
Escondido, CA 92027

714 4th Street
Eureka, CA 95501

1649 Van Ness Avenue
Fresno, CA 93721

Greenbriar Plaza
12912 Brookhurst Boulevard
Garden Grove, CA 92640

555 Redondo Beach Boulevard
Torrance, CA 90248

6022 Santa Fe Avenue
Huntington Park, CA 90255

83-558 Avenue 45, Suite 8
Indio, CA 92201

1671 Wilshire Blvd,
Los Angeles, CA 90017

1241 So. Soto Street
Los Angeles, CA 90022

11307 Vanowen Street
North Hollywood, CA 91605

400 S. "A" Street
Oxnard, CA 93030

60 East Holt Avenue
Pomona, CA 91767

1401 Gold Steet
Redding, CA 96001

1285 Columbia Avenue
Riverside, CA 92507

3041 65th Street
Sacramento, CA 95820-9000

947 Blanco Circle
Salinas, CA 93901

3247 Mission Village Drive
San Diego, CA 92123

Appraisers Building
630 Sansome Street
San Francisco, CA 94111

1727 Mission Street
San Francisco, CA 94103-2417

1040 Commercial Street
San Jose, CA 95112

1901 S. Ritchey Street
Santa Ana, CA 99501

16921 Parthenia Street
Sepulveda, CA 91343

7475 Murray Drive
Stockton, CA 95210

COLORADO

Albrook Center
4730 Paris Street
Denver, CO 80239

Enterprise Building
255 Main Street
Grand Junction, CO 81501

220 South Victoria Street
Pueblo, CO 81003

CONNECTICUT

414 Chapel Street
New Haven, CT 06511

FLORIDA

799 Galiano Street
Coral Gables, FL 33134

Jackson Building
601 S. Andrews Ave.
Fort Lauderdale, FL 33301

Federal Building
400 W. Bay Street
P.O.BOX 35044
Jacksonville, FL 32202

Rotunda Plaza
18922 S. Dixie Highway
Miami, FL 33157

North Lake Business Park
2900 Southwest Third Terrace
Okeechobee, FL 33974

Corporate Square, Suite 625
7402 N. 56th Street
Tampa, FL 33617

GEORGIA

1395 Columbia Drive, Suite A-10
Decatur, GA 30032

GUAM

801 Pacific News Building
238 O'Hara Street
Agana, GU 96910

HAWAII

1680 Kapiolani Boulevard
Honolulu, HI 96814

IDAHO

Stout Building II
1828 Airport Way
Boise, ID 83705

Exchange Plaza Building
1820 E. 17th Street
Idaho Falls, ID 83401

ILLINOIS

Farmsworth Center for Business
1050 Corporate Boulevard
Aurora, IL 60504

3119 North Pulaski
Chicago, IL 60641

Crown Oaks Midwest
Ground Floor
1700 W. 119th Street
Chicago, IL 60643

Forest Park Mall—Lower Level
7600 West Roosevelt Road
Forest Park, IL 60130

INDIANA

College Park Pyramids
3500 DePauw Boulevard
Indianapolis, IN 46268

IOWA

2720 W. Locust Street,
Suite 14
Davenport, IA 52804

3619½ Douglas Street
Des Moines, IA 50310

KANSAS

Forest Park Building
2506 John Street
Garden City, KS 67846

540 South Water
Wichita, KS 67202

LOUISIANA

512 South Peters
New Orleans, LA 70130

MAINE

156 Federal Street
Portland, ME 04101

MARYLAND

U.S. Appraisors Stores
Gay and Lombard Street
2nd Floor
Baltimore, MD 21202

MASSACHUSETTS

600 Washington Street
Boston, MA 02111

1149 Main Street
Springfield, MA 01103

MICHIGAN

15160 W. Eight Mile Road
Oak Park, MI 48327

MINNESOTA

Alpha Business Center
2700 East 82nd Street
Bloomington, MN 55420

MISSOURI

3445 Bridgeland Drive, Suite 123
Bridgeton, MO 63044

10336 NW Prairie View Road
Kansas City, MO 64153

MONTANA

Professional Plaza Building
900 North Montana
Helena, MT 59601

NEBRASKA

Bennett Building
1437 Tenth Street
Gering, NE 69341

River City Office Building
399 N. 117 Street, Suite 411
Omaha, NE 68154

NEW JERSEY

30 North 5th Street
Camden, NJ 08101

2853-2857 J.F. Kennedy Boulevard
Jersey City, NJ 07306

Franklin Mill Office Center
22 Mills Street
Paterson, NJ 07501

NEW MEXICO

1900 Bridge Boulevard, S.W.
Albuquerque, NM 87105

NEW YORK

Ansonia Center
712 Main Street at Tupper
Buffalo, NY 14202

250 Fulton Avenue
Hempstead, NY 11550

VA Federal Building
201 West 24th Street, 3rd Floor
New York, NY 10001

28-10 Queens Bridge Plaza South
Long Island City, NY 11101

344 West Genesee
Syracuse, NY 13202

NEVADA

3055 So. Valley View Boulevard
Las Vegas, NV 89102

350 S. Rock Boulevard, Unit "B"
Reno, NV 89502

NORTH CAROLINA

Highland Park Commerce Center
810 Tyvola Road, Suite 132
Charlotte, NC 28217

OHIO

100 E. Eighth Street
Cincinnati, OH 45202

Anthony J. Celebreeze Federal Building
1240 E. Ninth Street
Cleveland, OH 44199

OKLAHOMA

West Park Business Center
4149 Highline Boulevard, Suite 300
Oklahoma City, OK 73108

OREGON

AT&T Building
202 S.E. Dorion Street
Pendleton, OR 97801

Federal Building
511 N.W. Broadway
Portland, OR 97209

PENNSYLVANIA

Fair Acres Center
Route 352
Lima, PA 19037

Moorehead Federal Building
1000 Liberty Avenue
Third Floor–Room 314
Pittsburgh, PA 15222

PUERTO RICO

1609 Ponce De Leon
Santurce, PR 00908

TENNESSEE

147 Jefferson Avenue
Memphis, TN 38103

TEXAS

2001 E. Division
Arlington, TX 76011

2800 South Interstate 25, Suite 115
Austin, TX 78704

Commerce 2
4410 Dillon Lane
Corpus Christi, TX 78415

7028 Alameda Ave.
Lakeside Shopping Center
El Paso, TX 79915

603 Ed Carey Drive
Harlingen, TX 78550

2974 Fulton
Houston, TX 77009

2331 Saunders Plaza
Laredo, TX 78043

1940 Avenue G
Lubbock, TX 79404

Alta Vista Retail Center
1007 Poteet Jourdanton Freeway
San Antonio, TX 78224

UTAH

2990 South Main Street
Salt Lake City, UT 84115

VERMONT

Federal Building
P.O. Box 328
St. Albans, VT 05478

VIRGINIA

1521 N. Danville Street, 1st Floor
Arlington, VA 22201

WASHINGTON

430 West Lewis Street
P.O. Box 1336
Pasco, WA 99301

815 Airport Way South
Seattle, WA 98134

Como Solicitar la Naturalización

Si usted ha solicitado la ciudadanía, se pondrán a prueba sus conocimientos sobre la historia y el sistema americano de gobierno. También se someterán a prueba sus habilidades para leer, escribir y hablar el idioma inglés. Sin embargo, usted estará exento de esta última obligación si llena los siguientes requisitos: 1) Si para el 24 de diciembre de 1952, usted era mayor de 50 años de edad; 2) Si para esa fecha, usted había residido en los Estados Unidos durante un período mínimo de 20 años. Personas que estén físicamente incapacitadas para leer, escribir o hablar, también están exentas de tomar esta parte de la prueba.

REQUISITOS GENERALES PARA LA NATURALIZACION

Cada solicitante tiene que cumplir con todos los requisitos necesarios para la Naturalización, excepto que se encuentre en una categoría especial y quede exento de algunos de estos requisitos. Investigue en la oficina más cercana del Servicio de Inmigración y Naturalización para que se entere en qué categoría lo han clasificado a usted.

PRESENTANDO LA SOLICITUD

El primer paso es conseguir el formulario para presentar la solicitud y, excepto en casos de niños menores de 14 años de edad, la tarjeta para estampar sus huellas digitales y el modelo para suministrar la información biográfica que se requiere; todos estos patrones pueden obtenerse gratis en la oficina más cercana del Servicio de Inmigración y Naturalización. Si lo prefiere, usted puede llamar por teléfono, solicitarlos y recibir por correo todos estos formularios.

Si la solicitud es para usted, el patrón que debe usar es el Formulario N-400, "Solicitud para Presentar la Petición de Naturalización." Sin embargo, si un padre desea presentar una petición de naturalización en nombre de su hijo menor de edad, o de un niño que ha adoptado, entonces la solicitud que debe usar es el Formulario N-402, "Solicitud para Presentar la Petición de Naturalización en nombre de un Hijo."

Todos estos formularios tienen que ser llenados *exactamente según las instrucciones* que aparecen impresas en dichos patrones, y deben ser llevados, o enviados por correo, a las oficinas más cercanas del Servicio de Inmigración y Naturalización. Juntamente con estos formularios usted tiene que enviar tres fotografías, según se explica en la solicitud.

ESTUDIO DE LA SOLICITUD

Después que le hayan dado curso a la solicitud, el Servicio de Inmigración y Naturalización le informará que se ha señalado una cita entre usted y un Examinador, con el propósito de estudiar más a fondo su solicitud. El Examinador lo ayudará a usted a radicar los documentos legales—conocidos como "Petición de Naturalización"—ante el Tribunal de Naturalización.

LA AUDIENCIA FINAL

Una vez que se ha hecho el estudio y que la Petición ha sido radicada, usted deberá esperar por los menos 30 días antes de que se celebre la audiencia final ante el Tribunal de Naturalización. Con frecuencia, el juez no le formula preguntas; sin embargo, es de persona precavida ir debidamente preparada para poder contestar bien aquellas preguntas que a usted le han dicho podrían hacerle. Cuando no se formulan preguntas, el Examinador de Naturalización le informa al juez que usted ha sido encontrado calificado para la Naturalización, y que se le debe conceder la ciudadanía.

Cuando el Tribunal decide que usted es elegible para adquirir la ciudadanía, entonces usted tiene que prestar un Juramento de Fidelidad a los Estados Unidos. Al hacerlo, usted deshace los lazos de fidelidad con su antiguo país y promete apoyar y defender la Constitución y las leyes de los Estados Unidos.

ALGUNOS CONSEJOS QUE USTED DEBE RECORDAR CUANDO SE ENCUENTRE ANTE EL EXAMINADOR O ANTE EL TRIBUNAL

Nunca llegue tarde a su cita. Si llega aunque sea unos pocos minutos tarde para el estudio de su solicitud, usted perderá su turno y entonces tendrá que esperar hasta que le remitan una nueva cita por correo.

Si usted es hombre, lleve puesto chaquetón y corbata; y si usted es mujer, lleve puesto traje completo. EN TODO CASO, ¡NO SE VISTA CON ESA ROPA DE ALGODÓN CRUZADO QUE SE USA PARA "JEANS" O MAHONES! Usted debe vestirse como manda la ocasión, si puede.

Recuerde: siempre que se comunique con el Servicio de Inmigración y Naturalización, indique su número de inscripción como extranjero, y traiga con usted su tarjeta cuando venga a la audiencia. Usted deberá entregarla a uno de los Examinadores antes de recibir su Certificado de Naturalización. Si necesita más información, usted puede conseguir listas de las distintas oficinas del Servicio de Inmigración y Naturalización en su directorio telefónico local. Estas oficinas se encuentran bajo el encabezamiento de "*United States Government*." Si no puede encontrar la lista que busca, entonces marque el número telefónico "411" y pídale a la telefonista que le proporcione la *información* que usted necesita.

History of the United States

Europeans came to America soon after its discovery. The Spanish began exploring Mexico, Central America, and parts of North America as early as 1510. Ponce de León landed on the east coast of Florida a few years later.

England sent a number of expeditions to explore the new world, largely on the east coast of North America. One man, Sir Walter Raleigh, led several expeditions and named the land he explored "Virginia," in honor of Elizabeth I, the Virgin Queen. But it was after the death of Elizabeth that a full-scale effort to establish English colonies in the New World began. This effort came from merchants—not from the new King, James I.

The first large group of settlers to leave England came here in 1620 for religious reasons. About 100 people set out from Plymouth, England, on a ship named the *Mayflower*. The ship landed in America on Cape Cod Bay. The settlers decided to remain, and claimed to be free of English law. Before going ashore, the Pilgrims drew up what they called the Mayflower Compact:

> We whose names are underwritten, do by these present, solemnly and mutually in the presence of God and one another covenant and combine ourselves under . . . into a civil body politic . . . and by virtue hereof do enact . . . such just and equal laws . . . as shall be thought must meet and convene for the general good of the colony.

This group of religious dissenters had, in their simple way, created a new government, with no laws controlling religious beliefs. In 1791 this declaration of freedom from religious persecution became part of the Constitution of the United States. English merchants continued to encourage emigration to the New World, and between 1660 and 1760 England had established 13 colonies in North America.

Settlers from other nations arrived—French, Irish, German, Dutch, and many others. With them came new cultures and life-styles. These people became the first Americans.

During this period of colonization, between 1660 and 1760, most colonists continued to look to England for leadership. The northern colonies (Pennsylvania, New York, and New England) became more commercially inclined, while the South remained agricultural. Farming was hard and expensive. This and other problems with white labor contributed to the shift toward the use of slaves. By 1740, there were about 150,000 slaves in the South.

Meanwhile, the thirteen colonies were growing and the people were, to a large extent, independent from the king. During this time, Europe was continually at war and many immigrants came here to avoid being drafted. But there was little fighting in the New World until 1752, when the French and English clashed. Peace came in 1763, and the French abandoned their claims to North America except for two small islands in the St. Lawrence River. Canada became another of England's possessions at this time.

Because of the need for more revenue, England now began to tighten its control in the colonies. The continued warring on the Continent as well as the war to drive the French out of America and Canada had been expensive, and the colonies were expected to help the economy by paying more taxes. Trouble broke out between the colonists and the British Army. Some Americans sought independence from England. In June 1774, Massachusetts called for the first meeting of delegates from the 13 colonies to take action. They agreed, and in September, the First Continental Congress met in Philadelphia, with only Georgia absent.

The Revolutionary War

In January 1775, England ordered armed troops to fire upon the citizens who were in revolt in Massachusetts. This armed action by England quickly rallied the other colonies to the cause of freedom. The American Revolution had begun.

The Continental Congress named George Washington, who had served as commander in chief of the Virginia militia, to command the Continental forces. On July 4, 1776, with the help of Thomas Jefferson, Benjamin Franklin, John Adams, Roger Sherman, and Robert Livingston, the new Congress adopted the Declaration of Independence. In March 1781, the Articles of Confederation had been ratified, and in 1783 the signing of the Treaty of Paris officially ended the seven-year American Revolutionary War. The new country had won its independence from England. General George Washington was a national hero; he is now called "The Father of our Country."

The new country struggled to establish a new government. England and Spain were still in control of the land beyond the 13 colonies, and the Indians threatened the peace. America was young and weak. The 13 states had problems with the economy; the national government was not able to pay its debts.

The founding fathers called for a convention to change the Articles of Confederation. They altered the loose confederation of the former 13 colonies into a federated form, with a national government holding many of the powers once controlled by the states. That required consent by all the states. The meeting took place in Philadelphia. Delaware ratified in December, 1787, North Carolina in November, 1789, and Rhode Island held out until May, 1790. The first election took place between January and February of 1789, with George Washington the unanimous choice as the first president of the United States. John Adams won the Vice-Presidency.

On April 30, 1789, Washington took the Oath of Office. The problems with France, England, and Spain continued until 1794. Finally, on June 24, 1795, George Washington submitted to the senate a treaty with England, worked out by Chief Justice John Jay. It is called Jay's Treaty. This improved relations with England and helped the new nation grow without fear of war.

Without this danger, the United States began to expand. The Mississippi was now opened and the West was also, with the

Louisiana Purchase from France and the explorations of Lewis and Clark. Other explorations followed and brought back information about the size and resources of this new land. This was a period of expansion for the United States; unfortunately, wars with Indian tribes resulted. In 1812, war was again declared between the United States and England over freedom of the seas. The war was ended by the Treaty of Ghent in December 1814.

The country was again on the move towards prosperity, progress, and expansion. By 1820 the country had achieved major economic growth. In March 1836 Texas declared its independence from Mexico. In April, Sam Houston attacked the Mexican Army (led by General Santa Anna) and drove the Mexican Army out of Texas. He was elected President of the Republic of Texas. However, Texas was to join the United States after a short period of being a separate nation.

War between the United States and Mexico was declared in 1846. As a result of the conflict, Mexico lost part of California and New Mexico. With expansion, the question of slavery came up once again, North and South opposing each other on the issue.

As the United States grew larger and richer, the North became more industrialized, while the South remained almost totally agricultural. Because of this, the South needed cheap labor and continued to depend on slaves.

The Civil War

In the election of 1860, Abraham Lincoln became the 16th President of the United States. Slavery concerned Lincoln deeply. His election caused the South to threaten to secede from the Union. Shortly after Lincoln's election, the South and the North declared war upon each other; the Civil War began in 1861 and ended in 1865. Slavery was officially abolished in the Confederate States of America by the Emancipation Proclamation (Jan. 1, 1863).

The 11 Southern states were brought back into the Union. Americans now had to forget war and try to reunite the country.

By 1893 the United States had become an industrial giant.

Railroads, iron, oil, and electricity had changed the country into a great power and a world leader.

The Spanish-American War, 1898

Cuban rebels had been waging guerrilla warfare against Spain for many years. The United States wanted to oust the Spanish from Cuba, and in April 1898 Congress voted to recognize Cuba as an independent nation. American forces were sent to drive out the Spanish. Commodore George Dewey was ordered to move against the Spanish navy in the Philippine Islands (another Spanish possession); he defeated the Spanish fleet. Commodore Dewey asked for troops to be sent to hold Manila. In August, President William McKinley dispatched troops and Manila was captured. Meanwhile, Colonel Theodore Roosevelt was sent to Cuba; the Spanish surrendered on July 17. Puerto Rico and Guam, other Spanish possessions, became Territories of the United States. The Philippines were added, as well. In 1901, after a bitter fight between the United States and the Philippines, Congress allowed the islands to have their own civilian government. In July 1901 William Howard Taft became the first civilian Governor of the Philippines. In 1902 the United States pulled its troops out of Cuba, Puerto Rico, and Guam. Cuba became independent, but Puerto Rico and Guam remained United States Territories.

The Progressive Era

This period lasted from 1902 until America entered World War I. The Progressive Era was so called because of its relatively liberal outlook. The Seventeenth Amendment was adopted in 1913; this meant that United States Senators were no longer appointed but now elected by the people of each state.

Women were gaining support in their fight for the right to vote. However, this would not become a fact until 1920. The Anti-Trust Act was passed, making it illegal for large companies to band together and control one industry. Child labor laws were passed, and some protection was guaranteed workers in dangerous occupations. Public health became a legislative consideration, as well.

World War I—1914 to 1918

The United States had no wish to enter the war between Germany (and its allies) and France and Britain (and their allies). However, the sinking of the Lusitania in 1915 and the loss of freedom of the seas forced the United States into the war in 1917. Armistice was declared on November 11, 1918. The war had ended and the American people were ready to resume normal life.

Industrial output doubled from 1921 to 1929. But vast overextension of credit by the government and the public took its toll. On October 24, 1929, "Black Thursday", the stock market fell. This was the beginning of the Great Depression, which lasted from 1929 to 1939.

A New War Begins—World War II

When Germany invaded Poland in September 1939, Britain honored its treaty with Poland and declared war on Germany. There was little fighting during 1939. But in May of 1940, Germany altered events by first attacking Holland, Belgium, and Luxembourg, and then marching into France. In 1941 Germany invaded Russia. On December 7, 1941, the Japanese attacked Pearl Harbor, and war was declared on Japan and its allies by the United States. A peace treaty was signed in Europe in early 1945, but the war continued in the Pacific until the United States dropped its atom bomb on Hiroshima. Three days later, a second bomb hit Nagasaki. The Japanese surrendered on August 15, 1945. Following the end of World War II, the United States began, once again, to shift the economy from wartime back to peacetime.

Relations with America's former ally, Russia, gradually became strained. Historians call this unfriendly state of affairs the Cold War, due largely to Russia's and America's attempts to exert influence in the same areas. The economy thrived, unemployment was low, and business was booming. This boom in the economy and new peace was shattered in 1950 when North Koreans rumbled across the 38th parallel, which divided North and South Korea. American and United Nations troops fought the North Koreans until 1953. American troops remain in South Korea to this date.

Dwight D. Eisenhower became President in 1953. The economy was prosperous during the eight years Eisenhower was in office. One of the issues during his administration was Civil Rights; segregation in the Armed Forces was abolished at this time. But it was not until the Kennedy administration that stricter enforcement of Civil Rights became effective.

By August 1964, the United States was once again at war. In the early years of the Vietnamese War (from 1965 to 1967), about 165,000 American troops were fighting the Communists. By 1968, over 600,000 Americans were fighting. The war ended in January 1973. President Richard M. Nixon took credit for having ended the war.

The Nixon administration is a dark page in the history of the United States. During the investigation of the Watergate scandals, many officials called for his impeachment and resignation. His Vice President, Spiro T. Agnew, was accused of having accepted bribes when he was previously Governor of Maryland. Agnew resigned as Vice President and Nixon appointed Gerald R. Ford as Vice President, under the authority of the 25th Amendment. Meanwhile, the Watergate investigation continued. On August 8, 1974, Nixon announced his resignation. The next day, on August 9, 1974, Gerald Ford became the 38th President of the United States.

In the election of 1976, James (Jimmy) Carter defeated Ford for the presidency of the United States and became the 39th President. In 1980 Ronald Reagan defeated Carter and became the 40th President of this country.

America in the 1980s is faced with many problems, but it is hoped that American technology, know-how, and determination will see a new beginning of the American dream.

(Note: The reader must remember that this short history is designed to meet the requirements for persons seeking to pass the necessary tests to become naturalized citizens of the United States. It is not meant to replace textbooks used in school.)

Historia de los Estados Unidos

Los europeos vinieron a América poco después de su descubrimiento. Al despuntar el siglo XVI, los españoles comenzaron a explorar partes de lo que hoy es México, América Central y Estados Unidos de América del Norte. Ponce de León cruzaba la costa oriental de Florida pocos años más tarde, en 1513.

Inglaterra envió numerosas expediciones a explorar el Nuevo Mundo, principalmente rumbo a la costa atlántica de América del Norte. En esta zona, Sir Walter Raleigh, que dirigió varias expediciones, estableció un poblado que englobaba todo el litoral al norte de Florida, al que llamó "Virginia," en honor a la reina Isabel I. Sin embargo, fue después de la muerte de Isabel I que comenzó un esfuerzo sistemático para fundar colonias inglesas en la costa atlántica de los Estados Unidos. Este gran esfuerzo no se debió a la iniciativa del nuevo rey, Jaime I, sino al empeño de los mercaderes.

En 1620 vino a América el primer grupo numeroso de colonos ingleses, unas cien personas, entre hombres y mujeres. Se les conoce como *Peregrinos* y venían en búsqueda de libertad para sus creencias religiosas. Este grupo vino en el velero "Mayflower," que partió del puerto de Plymouth, Inglaterra, y llegó el 11 de diciembre a la bahía de Cape Cod, Massachusetts, que vino a ser el segundo asentamiento británico en el Nuevo Mundo. Antes de desembarcar, los Peregrinos redactaron el documento que ellos llamaron El Pacto del Mayflower:

> Nosotros, los que subscribimos, ante Dios y ante unos a otros, por este medio, solemne y recíprocamente hacemos un pacto y nos unimos bajo . . . en un cuerpo político civil . . . y en virtud de esto decretamos . . . aquellas leyes justas e imparciales . . . que como se ha pensado tienen que responder y convenir más al bien general de la colonia.

Así, de una manera sencilla, acorde con su modo de vida, este grupo de disidentes religiosos había creado un nuevo sistema de gobierno, sin leyes que restringieran las creencias religiosas. En 1791, esta aserción de la libertad de culto se convirtió en parte de la Constitución de los Estados Unidos.

Los mercaderes ingleses continuaron estimulando la emigración al Nuevo Mundo, y entre 1660 y 1760 Inglaterra había fundado 13 colonias en América del Norte.

Llegaron también inmigrantes de otras nacionalidades—franceses, irlandeses, alemanes, holandeses, y de muchos otros países. Con ellos, llegaron nuevas culturas y modos de vida. Andando el tiempo, estos colonos vinieron a convertirse en los primeros americanos.

Durante este período de la colonización, la mayoría de los colonos seguían mirando hacia Inglaterra en busca de dirección para encauzar sus pasos. Las colonias del norte (Pennsylvania, New York y New England) se inclinaron más hacia el comercio, mientras que las del sur continuaron dedicadas a la agricultura. El cultivo de la tierra era una tarea dura y costosa. Este factor y otros problemas surgidos con los trabajadores blancos, contribuyeron a la decisión de hacer uso de esclavos negros. Para 1740 había alrededor de 150,000 esclavos en el Sur.

Mientras tanto, las 13 colonias estaban creciendo y la gente era, en amplio grado, independiente de la Corona inglesa. Durante todo este período, Europa estuvo continuamente enfrascada en guerras y fueron muchos los inmigrantes que vinieron a América con el fin de evitar ser reclutados en los ejércitos beligerantes. En el Nuevo Mundo, por el contrario, hubo muy pocas luchas hasta 1752, cuando chocaron los franceses y los ingleses. Los colonos se mantuvieron leales a Inglaterra en las guerras que ésta sostuvo con Francia en América y que culminaron con la derrota definitiva de los franceses (1759–60) y el Tratado de París (1763) que puso fin al imperio colonial francés en Norteamérica. A la vez, Canadá vino a convertirse en otra posesión de Inglaterra.

Las guerras continuas en Europa, así como los combates para expulsar a los franceses de América y Canadá, habían resultado costosos y el Rey quería que las colonias aumentaran sus contribuciones a la economía inglesa. Surgieron algunos disturbios entre colonos y soldados británicos. Algunos americanos aspiraban a independizarse de Inglaterra. En junio de 1774, a fin de tomar una determinación sobre la acción a seguir, Massachusetts convocó a la primera reunión de delegados de las 13 colonias.

El Primer Congreso Continental se reunió en Filadelfia (Philadelphia), en septiembre de ese mismo año, para elevar al Parlamento de Londres un memorial de agravios. Sólo Georgia estuvo ausente. Los colonos protestaban contra los pesados impuestos y las restricciones comerciales que entorpecían el desarrollo económico de las colonias.

La Guerra de Independencia, 1776–1783

En enero de 1775, Inglaterra dio órdenes a sus tropas de que abrieran fuego contra la gente que se había rebelado en Massachusetts. Este hecho de armas por parte de Inglaterra estimuló inmediatamente a las otras colonias a cerrar filas en defensa de la libertad. La Revolución Americana había comenzado.

En mayo de 1775, el Segundo Congreso Continental, reunido en Filadelfia, declaró la guerra a Inglaterra y designó a George Washington, que era un Coronel del Ejército Continental, para dirigir las tropas insurgentes.

Al año siguiente (4 de Julio), con la participación de Thomas Jefferson, Benjamin Franklin, John Adams, Roger Sherman, Robert Livingston y otros próceres, el Congreso promulgó la Declaración de Independencia.

Terminada la Guerra de Independencia, o Guerra de la Revolución, Inglaterra reconoció la soberanía de los Estados Unidos por el tratado de paz firmado en París en 1783. El General George Washington era un héroe nacional. Hoy se le conoce como "El Padre de nuestro País".

En 1777 el Congreso Continental había redactado unos "Artículos de Confederación", que fueron ratificados en 1781. En ellos se anunciaba una firme liga de amistad y unión perpetua entre los 13 Estados, aunque cada uno seguía en pleno uso de su soberanía. Este sistema, sin embargo, llevaba a la anarquía: El Congreso creaba leyes que no podía poner en vigor. No había Presidente, ni cortes de justicia. Los Estados reñían entre sí. La Unión estaba en peligro.

El nuevo país luchaba por organizar un sistema de gobierno más eficaz. Inglaterra y España todavía dominaban las tierras allende a las 13 colonias, y los indios indígenas del país amenazaban la paz. América era joven y débil. Los 13 Estados tenían problemas con sus respectivas economías; y el gobierno nacional no podía saldar sus deudas, ya que el Congreso no tenía poderes para imponer tributos.

El Congreso solicitó a los Estados que enviaran delegados a una convención para cambiar los Artículos de Confederación. Todos los Estados, excepto Rhode Island, enviaron delegaciones. A esta reunión, convocada para organizar un nuevo sistema de gobierno, se le llamó la Convención Constituyente. Comenzó el 25 de mayo de 1787, en Filadelfia. Los delegados eligieron a George Washington para presidir los trabajos de la Convención.

Los delegados llegaron a la conclusión de que era imposible cambiar los Artículos de Confederación; de que era necesario estructurar un sistema de gobierno completamente nuevo, y comenzaron a elaborar uno.

El 17 de septiembre de 1787, los delegados terminaron sus labores, y firmaron el nuevo plan. La Convención solicitó que todos los Estados eligieran delegados, para que éstos emitieran su voto sobre la nueva Constitución. La Constitución que ellos expidieron es la misma que hoy rige y se adoptó oficialmente el 21 de junio de 1788, al completarse su ratificación por 9 Estados. Washington, electo Presidente de la nación, tomó posesión en New York, el 30 de abril de 1789. John Adams fue electo Vice Presidente. Había comenzado sus funciones el primer gobierno verdadero de los Estados Unidos.

Sin embargo, los problemas con Francia, Inglaterra y España continuaron hasta 1794. Finalmente, el 24 de junio de 1795, Washington sometió ante la consideración del Senado un Tratado que estaba siendo negociado con Inglaterra. Dicho Tratado había sido preparado por John Jay, el Juez Presidente de la Corte Suprema. El Senado lo aprobó. Su ratificación mejoró las relaciones entre ambos países y ayudó a la nueva nación a crecer sin el peligro de un nuevo conflicto bélico.

Sin la amenaza de una guerra, los Estados Unidos comenzó a expandirse. En 1803, durante la presidencia de Thomas Jefferson, Estados Unidos le compró a Francia el territorio de Luisiana (Louisiana), que abarca casi toda la región situada entre el Río Misisipí y las Montañas Rocosas. El Misisipí era ahora accesible y también quedaba libre el camino hacia el Oeste. Comenzaron a llevarse a cabo una serie de exploraciones, que proporcionaron datos de gran importancia sobre la extensión y los recursos naturales de esta nueva tierra. Este fue un período de expansión para los Estados Unidos, pero, desafortunadamente, vino a parar en las guerras con las tribus indias. En 1812, nuevamente hubo guerra entre Estados Unidos e Inglaterra, esta vez con motivo de la libertad de los mares. La guerra terminó con el tratado de paz de Gante, en 1814.

El país estaba nuevamente en camino hacia la expansión, el progreso y la prosperidad. Para 1820, el país había alcanzado un crecimiento económico de considerable importancia. En marzo de 1836, Texas declaró su independencia de México. En abril, Sam Houston atacó al ejército mexicano, expulsando de Texas a las tropas comandadas por el General Santa Ana. Houston fue electo Presidente de la República de Texas. Después de unos años como nación independiente, Texas fue admitida como un Estado de la Unión, en 1845.

En 1846, se declaró la guerra entre Estados Unidos y México. Como resultado de ese conflicto, Mexico perdió California y Nuevo México. La guerra terminó en 1848. Con la expansión territorial, volvió a resurgir el problema de la esclavitud. Los Estados del Norte y los del Sur mantenían posiciones opuestas con respecto a esta cuestión.

Según los Estados Unidos se fue haciendo más grande y más rico, los Estados del Norte se fueron industrializando, mientras que los del Sur siguieron siendo casi totalmente agrícolas. Debido a esta condición, el Sur necesitaba mano de obra barata y por esta razon continuó dependiendo del trabajo esclavo.

La Guerra Civil 1861–1865

La expansión hacia el Oeste había planteado una pugna

irreconciliable entre los esclavistas del Sur, que aspiraban a extender su sistema a los nuevos Estados, y los norteños, partidarios de la abolición de la esclavitud.

En las elecciones de 1860, Abraham Lincoln fue electo como el décimosexto Presidente de los Estados Unidos. La esclavitud preocupaba profundamente a Lincoln. Al resultar éste electo, los Estados sureños comenzaron a separarse de la Unión. Había empezado la Guerra de Secesión o Civil, que duró desde 1861 hasta 1865. El lro. de enero de 1863, Lincoln emitió la Proclama de Emancipación, aboliendo la esclavitud en los Estados Confederados del Sur. Dos años más tarde, la Décimotercera Enmienda dio oficialmente fin al régimen esclavista en los Estados Unidos.

Los once Estados sureños fueron reintegrados a la Unión. Los americanos ahora tenían que olvidar la guerra y dedicarse a reconstruir el país.

Para 1893, los Estados Unidos ya se había convertido en un gigante industrial. Los ferrocarriles, el hierro, el petróleo, la electricidad y las fábricas habían transformado el país en una gran potencia y guía, a nivel mundial.

La Guerra Hispano-Americana, 1898

Durante muchos años, los patriotas cubanos habían venido librando una guerra de guerrillas contra España; luchaban por la independencia. Estados Unidos quería expulsar a los españoles de Cuba y, en abril de 1898, el Congreso reconoció a Cuba como una nación independiente. Las fuerzas armadas americanas fueron enviadas a arrojar a los españoles de sus últimas posesiones en el Nuevo Mundo. El Comodoro George Dewey recibió órdenes de atacar la flota española en las Islas Filipinas, y la destruyó. Dewey pidió que se enviaran tropas para tomar Manila, la capital. En agosto, el Presidente William McKinley envió las tropas y Manila fue tomada. Mientras tanto, el Coronel Theodore Roosevelt había sido enviado a Cuba, donde los españoles se rindieron el 17 de julio. Puerto Rico y Guam, que también eran posesiones de España, se convirtieron en Territorios de los Estados Unidos, al igual que las Filipinas.

En 1901, después de enconados combates entre tropas norteamericanas y filipinos independentistas, el Congreso le permitió a dichas islas tener su propio gobierno civil. En julio de ese mismo año, William H. Taft se convirtió en el primer Gobernador civil de Las Filipinas. En 1902, los Estados Unidos retiró sus tropas de Cuba, Puerto Rico y Guam. Cuba recibió su independencia pero Puerto Rico y Guam continuaron siendo Territorios de Estados Unidos.

La Era Progresista, 1902–1917

Este período se extiende desde 1902 hasta que América entra en la Primera Guerra Mundial. A estos años se les ha llamado así, por su perspectiva relativamente liberal. En 1913 se aprobó la Décimoséptima (17ma) Enmienda; ésta dispuso que los Senadores Federales no seguirían siendo nombrados, sino que de ahora en adelante serían electos por el pueblo, en cada Estado.

Las mujeres estaban ganando apoyo en su lucha para que se les reconociera el derecho al voto; sin embargo, este derecho no fue oficialmente reconocido hasta 1920. Se aprobó la Ley Contra los Monopolios (Anti-Trust Act), que declaraba ilegal el que las grandes empresas se amalgamaran con el fin de dominar por completo una industria o negocio. Se sancionaron estatutos que prohibían el empleo de menores de edad; y se garantizó alguna protección para los trabajadores ocupados en labores que constituían un peligro para quienes las desempeñaban. La Salud Pública, también, vino a convertirse en un asunto de interés legislativo.

Primera Guerra Mundial, 1914–1918

Estados Unidos no deseaba tomar parte en la guerra entre Alemania (y sus aliados) y Francia e Inglaterra (y sus aliados). Sin embargo, el hundimiento del Lusitania en 1915 y la pérdida de la libertad de los mares debido a la campaña submarina alemana, obligó a los Estados Unidos a cambiar de opinión. En 1917, América le declaró la guerra a Alemania. El 11 de noviembre de

1918 el Armisticio puso fin a la guerra. Los Aliados habían triunfado sobre las Potencias Centrales. Terminado el conflicto, el pueblo americano estaba listo para reanudar una vida normal.

La producción industrial fue duplicada entre 1921 y 1929. Sin embargo, el enorme agobio a que fue sometido el crédito, tanto por parte del público como por parte del gobierno, tuvo sus efectos desastrosos. El 24 de octubre de 1929, la Bolsa de Valores de New York se vino al suelo. Este fue el comienzo de la Gran Depresión, que duró desde 1929 hasta 1939.

Segunda Guerra Mundial, 1939–1945

Cuando Hitler invadió Polonia en septiembre de 1939, los ingleses cumplieron su pacto con los polacos, y Gran Bretaña le declaró la guerra a Alemania. Durante unos meses, el conflicto bélico no se generalizó. Sin embargo, en mayo de 1940, la guerra comenzó a extenderse rápidamente. Alemania atacó a Holanda, Bélgica y Luxemburgo, marchando luego sobre Francia. En 1941, Alemania invadió la Unión Soviética. El 7 de diciembre de 1941, los japoneses atacaron Pearl Harbor y los Estados Unidos le declaró la guerra a Japón. A principios de 1945, se firmó un tratado de paz en Europa, pero la guerra continuó en el Pacífico, hasta que Estados Unidos lanzó la bomba atómica, primero sobre Hiroshima, y luego sobre Nagasaki. Los japoneses se rindieron pocos días después, el 15 de agosto de 1945. Terminada la conflagración, Estados Unidos comenzó nuevamente a convertir una economía de guerra en una economía de paz.

Recién terminado el conflicto, las relaciones entre América y la Unión Soviética, que habían sido aliados durante la guerra, se volvieron tirantes. Los analistas llaman "Guerra Fría" a este estado de relaciones poco amistosas; estado provocado, en gran medida, por los intentos de América y la Unión Soviética de ejercer influencia sobre las mismas áreas. Durante este período, la economía mejoró, hubo poco desempleo y los negocios prosperaron. Sin embargo, esta prosperidad económica y la nueva paz fueron quebrantadas en 1950, cuando las tropas norcoreanas cruzaron el Paralelo 38, que es la línea divisoria entre Corea del Norte y Corea del Sur. El ejército americano y tropas de las Naciones Unidas combatieron con las fuerzas norcoreanas hasta 1953. Hasta el presente, las tropas americanas siguen estacionadas en Corea del Sur.

Dwight D. Eisenhower fue electo Presidente en 1953. La economía mejoró durante los ocho años de su administración. Uno de los puntos en cuestión durante la presidencia de Eisenhower fue el de los Derechos Civiles; como consecuencia, la segregación racial fue abolida en las Fuerzas Armadas. Sin embargo, no fue hasta la presidencia de John F. Kennedy en que se hizo un esfuerzo mayor para poner en vigor las leyes de Derechos Civiles.

En agosto de 1964, Estados Unidos estaba nuevamente en guerra. Durante los primeros años (1965–67) de la guerra en Vietnam, alrededor de 165,000 soldados americanos estaban combatiendo allí contra los comunistas; para 1968, el número había ascendido a más de medio millón. La guerra terminó en enero de 1973. El Presidente Richard M. Nixon recibió el crédito por haber logrado poner fin al conflicto.

Sin embargo, la administración de Nixon es una página sombría en la historia de los Estados Unidos. Durante la investigación del escándalo político de "Watergate," muchos funcionarios manifestaron su opinión de que Nixon debía ser residenciado ("impeached"), y demandaron su renuncia. El Vice Presidente, Spiro T. Agnew, fue acusado de haber aceptado sobornos cuando era Gobernador de Maryland. Agnew renunció y Nixon designó Vice Presidente a Gerald R. Ford, según estaba autorizado a hacerlo en virtud de la Vigésimaquinta (25ta) Enmienda. Mientras tanto, continuaba la investigación del Caso Watergate. El 8 de agosto de 1974, Nixon anunció su renuncia. Al día siguiente, Gerald Ford se convirtió en el trigésimoctavo (38vo) Presidente de los Estados Unidos.

En las elecciones presidenciales de 1976, James (Jimmy) Carter derrotó a Gerald Ford y se convirtió en el trigésimonoveno Presidente de los Estados Unidos. Jimmy Carter fue a su vez derrotado en las elecciones de 1980 por Ronald Reagan, quien es hoy en día Presidente de este país.

En la década de 1980, América tiene ante sí muchos problemas, pero se espera que su tecnología, su genio intuitivo y su determinación verán un nuevo comienzo del sueño americano.

(Nota: El lector debe recordar que esta es una historia sinóptica, escrita para preparar a aquellas personas que quieren pasar las pruebas necesarias para hacerse ciudadanos americanos. Esta breve historia no pretende substituir los libros de texto que se usan en las escuelas.)

United States Government

Federal, State, and Local

The Constitution of the United States is called the "highest law of the land." It gives power to the Federal and State governments, and protects the rights of citizens. There are three branches to the Federal government: executive, judicial, and legislative.

Like the Federal government, each State has three branches: executive, judicial, and legislative. However, the governmental systems of the individual states are not all the same, because each state has its own constitution.

In state government the Governor, Lieutenant Governor, Secretary of State, Attorney General, and other officials are the executive branch. The Governor, like the President, has his duties which are spelled out in each state constitution.

The judicial system is unique in every state. Most, however, have a Supreme Court and a Court of Criminal Appeals. Their decisions can be overruled by the Federal courts and the United States Supreme Court.

The legislative branch of government in a state may also be unique with regard to structure, size, and power. The laws are created by the State Legislature, but when doubts arise about a new law or the authority of the state's local government, the

El Gobierno de los Estados Unidos

FEDERAL, ESTATAL Y LOCAL

La Constitución de los Estados Unidos se conoce como "la ley suprema del país." La Constitución le confiere poderes a los gobiernos Federal y Estatal, y protege los derechos de los ciudadanos. El gobierno Federal consta de tres ramas: la ejecutiva, la legislativa y la judicial. Esta division del Poder Público en tres órganos fue consagrada por la Constitución.

Al igual que el gobierno Federal, el gobierno de cada Estado tiene tres ramas: ejecutiva, legislativa y judicial. Sin embargo, los sistemas de gobierno de los distintos Estados no son todos iguales, ya que cada Estado tiene su propia constitución estatal.

En el sistema de gobierno estatal, la rama ejecutiva está integrada por el Gobernador, el Vice Gobernador, el Secretario de Estado, el Procurador General y otros funcionarios. El Gobernador, al igual que el Presidente, tiene deberes que están claramente explicados en la constitución de cada Estado.

El sistema judicial de cada Estado es singular, o sea, característico de esa parte del país. Sin embargo, la mayoría cuentan con una Corte Suprema y una Corte Criminal de Apelaciones. Las decisiones de estos tribunales estatales pueden ser anuladas por las Cortes Federales y por la Corte Suprema de los Estados Unidos.

La rama legislativa en el sistema de gobierno estatal también puede ser singular o característica, con respecto a su estructura, tamaño y poder. Las leyes son creadas por cada Legislatura Estatal, pero cuando surgen dudas con respecto a la constitucionalidad de una nueva ley, o el grado de autoridad de que está investido el gobierno estatal local, son las cortes las que determinan si esos nuevos estatutos o esas atribuciones estatales están o

courts decide whether they conflict with the United States Constitution. State legislators deal mostly with local matters affecting the cities.

A Mayor and a City Council are found in most cities. The City Council is a single chamber and its size can vary. Some City Councils have two members, others have as many as 50 or more. They are elected by popular vote.

no en conflicto con la Constitución de los Estados Unidos. Los legisladores estatales se ocupan mayormente de cuestiones de tipo local, de asuntos que afectan directamente las distintas ciudades.

La mayoría de las ciudades cuentan con un Alcalde y un Concejo Municipal. El Concejo Municipal consiste de una sola cámara y su tamaño puede variar. Algunos Concejos consisten de sólo dos *Concejales,* y otros cuentan con 50, y hasta con más miembros. Los miembros del Concejo Municipal son elegidos por voto popular.

American History

Questions and Answers

1. *Q.* Name the 13 original colonies.
   A.
   1. Connecticut
   2. Delaware
   3. Georgia
   4. Maryland
   5. Massachusetts
   6. New Hampshire
   7. New Jersey
   8. New York
   9. North Carolina
   10. Pennsylvania
   11. Rhode Island
   12. South Carolina
   13. Virginia

2. *Q.* Who is called the "Father" of this country?
   A. George Washington.

3. *Q.* Who was the Commander-in-Chief of the American Army at the time of the Revolutionary War?
   A. George Washington.

4. *Q.* What do the stripes of the United States flag stand for?
   A. The original 13 states.

5. *Q.* What are the highest Mountains in the United States?
   A. The Rocky Mountains.

6. *Q.* Name the original 13 states.
   A.
   1. Connecticut
   2. Delaware
   3. Georgia
   4. Maryland
   5. Massachusetts
   6. New Hampshire
   7. New Jersey
   8. New York
   9. North Carolina
   10. Pennsylvania
   11. Rhode Island
   12. South Carolina
   13. Virginia

Historia de los Estados Unidos

Preguntas y Respuestas

1. *P.* Nombre las 13 colonias originales.
   R. 1. Connecticut
   2. Delaware
   3. Georgia
   4. Maryland
   5. Massachusetts
   6. New Hampshire
   7. New Jersey
   8. New York
   9. North Carolina
   10. Pennsylvania
   11. Rhode Island
   12. South Carolina
   13. Virginia

2. *P.* ¿A quién se la llama el "Padre" de esta país?
   R. George Washington.

3. *P.* ¿Quién era el Comandante-en-Jefe del Ejército Americano durante la Guerra de Independencia?
   R. George Washington.

4. *P.* ¿Qué significan las franjas de la bandera de los Estados Unidos?
   R. Los 13 Estados originales.

5. *P.* ¿Cuáles son las montañas más altas en los Estados Unidos?
   R. Las Montañas Rocosas.

6. *P.* Nombre los 13 Estados originales.
   R. 1. Connecticut
   2. Delaware
   3. Georgia
   4. Maryland
   5. Massachusetts
   6. New Hampshire
   7. New Jersey
   8. New York
   9. North Carolina
   10. Pennsylvania
   11. Rhode Island
   12. South Carolina
   13. Virginia

7. *Q.* Who was George Washington?
   A. He was the Commander-in-Chief of the American Army at the time of the Revolutionary War. He was also the first President of the United States.

8. *Q.* Who was Abraham Lincoln?
   A. He was the 16th President of the United States. He freed the slaves and saved the Union.

9. *Q.* What is the Declaration of Independence?
   A. It is a document signed by the delegates from the 13 colonies on July 4, 1776, declaring that they were free and independent from Britain.

10. *Q.* What was the Revolutionary War?
    A. It was the war between the 13 colonies and Britain over taxes and freedom. The colonies won the war.

11. *Q.* When was the Revolutionary War?
    A. From 1775 to 1783.

12. *Q.* What was the Civil War?
    A. It was the war between the North and the South over slavery and economics. The North won the war.

13. *Q.* When was the Civil War?
    A. From 1861 to 1865.

14. *Q.* What do the stars of the United States flag represent?
    A. Each star represents a state.

15. *Q.* What is the name of the national anthem?
    A. *The Star Spangled Banner.*

7. *P.* ¿Quién era George Washington?
   R. El Comandante-en-Jefe del Ejército Americano durante la Guerra de Independencia. También fue el primer Presidente de los Estados Unidos.

8. *P.* ¿Quién era Abraham Lincoln?
   R. El décimosexto (16to.) Presidente de los Estados Unidos. Lincoln emancipó los esclavos y salvó la Unión.

9. *P.* ¿Qué es la Declaración de Independencia?
   R. Es el documento en el que las 13 colonias se declararon libres e independientes de Inglaterra; fue promulgada por los Delegados el 4 de Julio de 1776.

10. *P.* ¿Qué fue la Guerra de la Revolución o Guerra de Independencia?
    R. Fue la guerra entre las 13 colonias e Inglaterra, a causa de los impuestos sin representación y el derecho a un gobierno representativo. Las colonias ganaron la guerra.

11. *P.* ¿Durante cuáles años se combatió en la Guerra de Independencia?
    R. Desde 1775 hasta 1783.

12. *P.* ¿Qué fue la Guerra Civil?
    R. Fue la guerra entre los Estados del norte y los del sur, a causa de la esclavitud y otros desacuerdos sobre economía, política. El Norte ganó la guerra.

13. *P.* ¿Durante cuáles años se combatió en la Guerra Civil?
    R. Desde 1861 hasta 1865.

14. *P.* ¿Qué representan las estrellas de la bandera de los Estados Unidos?
    R. Cada estrella representa un Estado.

15. *P.* ¿Cómo se llama el Himno Nacional?
    R. *The Star Spangled Banner* (Bandera Tachonada de Estrellas)

16. *Q.* What are the most important documents in the history of the United States?
    A. 1. The Declaration of Independence.
    2. The Articles of Confederation.
    3. The Constitution.
    4. The Emancipation Proclamation.

17. *Q.* Who were the Pilgrims?
    A. They were among the first settlers to come to this country seeking freedom of religion. They arrived in Massachusetts in 1620.

18. *Q.* Who wrote the Constitution?
    A. Delegates from the 13 colonies.

19. *Q.* What is the United States?
    A. It is a federated union of 50 states.

20. *Q.* What is the capital of the United States?
    A. Washington, D.C.

21. *Q.* How many states are there in the United States?
    A. There are 50 states.

22. *Q.* Where does the President live?
    A. He lives in the White House in Washington, D.C.

23. *Q.* Who was the first President of the United States?
    A. George Washington.

24. *Q.* Who was the 16th President of the United States?
    A. Abraham Lincoln.

25. *Q.* What is the longest river in the United States?
    A. It is the Mississippi River.

26. *Q.* How many stars are there in the United States flag?
    A. There are 50 stars.

16. *P.* ¿Cuáles son los documentos más importantes en la historia de los Estados Unidos?
R. 1. La Declaración de Independencia.
2. Los Artículos de Confederación.
3. La Constitución.
4. La Proclama de Emancipación.

17. *P.* ¿Quiénes eran los Peregrinos?
R. Los primeros colonos europeos que llegaron a este país, en búsqueda de libertad para sus creencias religiosas. Llegaron a Massachusetts en 1620.

18. *P.* ¿Quién redactó la Constitución?
R. Los delegados de las 13 colonias.

19. *P.* ¿Qué son los Estados Unidos?
R. Una federación integrada por 50 Estados.

20. *P.* ¿Cuál es la capital de los Estados Unidos?
R. Washington, D.C.

21. *P.* ¿Cuántos Estados componen a los Estados Unidos?
R. Hay 50 Estados.

22. *P.* ¿Dónde vive el Presidente?
R. En la Casa Blanca, en Washington, D.C.

23. *P.* ¿Quién fue el primer Presidente de los Estados Unidos?
R. George Washington.

24. *P.* ¿Quién fue el décimosexto (16to) Presidente de los Estados Unidos?
R. Abraham Lincoln.

25. *P.* ¿Cuál es el río más largo de los Estados Unidos?
R. El Río Misisipí (Mississippi).

26. *P.* ¿Cuántas estrellas hay en la bandera de los Estados Unidos?
R. Hay 50 estrellas.

27. *Q.* How many stripes are there in the United States flag?
    A. There are 13 stripes (7 red and 6 white).

28. *Q.* What is the 4th of July?
    A. It is Independence Day of the United States.

29. *Q.* Have you studied the United States Constitution?
    A. Yes, I have.

30. *Q.* What is the Constitution?
    A. It is the highest law of the United States.

31. *Q.* Do you know the meaning of the colors of the United States flag?
    A. Yes: red is for courage, white is for purity, and blue is for justice and truth.

32. *Q.* Who wrote *The Star Spangled Banner?*
    A. It was written in 1814 by Francis Scott Key, a Maryland lawyer, during the bombardment of Fort McHenry. It was adopted by Congress as the national anthem in 1931.

33. *Q.* Name the territorial expansions.
    A.

1. Louisiana Purchase	1803
2. Florida	1819
3. Texas	1845
4. Oregon	1846
5. Mexican Cession	1848
6. Gadsden Purchase	1853
7. Alaska	1867
8. Hawaii	1898
9. The Philippines	1898–1946

27. *P.* ¿Cuántas franjas tiene la bandera de los Estados Unidos?
R. Tiene 13 franjas (7 rojas y 6 blancas).

28. *P.* ¿Qué es el 4 de Julio?
R. Es el día en que se celebra la independencia de los Estados Unidos.

29. *P.* ¿Ha estudiado usted la Constitución de los Estados Unidos?
R. Sí, la he estudiado.

30. *P.* ¿Qué es la Constitución?
R. Es la ley suprema de los Estados Unidos.

31. *P.* ¿Sabe usted qué significan los colores de la bandera de los Estados Unidos?
R. Sí; el rojo, significa valor, el blanco, pureza, y el azul, justicia.

32. *P.* ¿Quién es el autor de la letra de *The Star Spangled Banner*?
R. Francis Scott Key, un abogado de Maryland, quien la escribió en 1814, durante el bombardeo del Fuerte McHenry. El Congreso la adoptó en 1931 como el Himno Nacional.

33. *P.* Nombre las expansiones territoriales.
R.

1. Compra del Territorio de Luisiana	1803
2. Florida	1819
3. Texas	1845
4. Oregón	1846
5. Cesión de México (Nuevo México, California, Arizona y Texas)	1848
6. Compra de Gadsden (zona del río Gila, en Arizona)	1853
7. Alaska	1867
8. Hawaii	1898
9. Las Filipinas	1898–1946

10. Puerto Rico	1898
11. Guam	1898
12. American Samoa	1900
13. Canal Zone	1904–1979
14. U.S. Virgin Islands	1917
15. Pacific Islands	1947
16. Trust Territory	1947

34. *Q.* Name the Presidents of the United States and give the years they were in office.

A.

1. George Washington	1789–1797
2. John Adams	1797–1801
3. Thomas Jefferson	1801–1809
4. James Madison	1809–1817
5. James Monroe	1817–1825
6. John Quincy Adams	1825–1829
7. Andrew Jackson	1829–1837
8. Martin Van Buren	1837–1841
9. William Henry Harrison	1841
10. John Tyler	1841–1845
11. James Knox Polk	1845–1849
12. Zachary Taylor	1849–1850
13. Millard Fillmore	1850–1853
14. Franklin Pierce	1853–1857
15. James Buchanan	1857–1861
16. Abraham Lincoln	1861–1865
17. Andrew Johnson	1865–1869
18. Ulysses Simpson Grant	1869–1877
19. Rutherford Birchard Hayes	1877–1881
20. James Abram Garfield	1881
21. Chester Alan Arthur	1881–1885
22. Grover Cleveland	1885–1889
23. Benjamin Harrison	1889–1893
24. Grover Cleveland	1893–1897
25. William McKinley	1897–1901

10.	Puerto Rico	1898
11.	Guam (en el Pacífico)	1898
12.	Samoa (en el Pacífico)	1900
13.	Zona del Canal de Panamá	1904–1979
14.	Islas Vírgenes	1917
15.	Islas del Pacífico	1947
16	Territorio en Fideicomiso (Islas Marianas [excepto Guam], Carolinas, Marshall)	1947

34. *P.* Nombre los Presidentes de los Estados Unidos y señale los años durante los cuales ejercieron dicho cargo.

R.

1.	George Washington	1789–1797
2.	John Adams	1797–1801
3.	Thomas Jefferson	1801–1809
4.	James Madison	1809–1817
5.	James Monroe	1817–1825
6.	John Quincy Adams	1825–1829
7.	Andrew Jackson	1829–1837
8.	Martin Van Buren	1837–1841
9.	William Henry Harrison	1841
10.	John Tyler	1841–1845
11.	James Knox Polk	1845–1849
12.	Zachary Taylor	1849–1850
13.	Millard Fillmore	1850–1853
14.	Franklin Pierce	1853–1857
15.	James Buchanan	1857–1861
16.	Abraham Lincoln	1861–1865
17.	Andrew Johnson	1865–1869
18.	Ulysses Simpson Grant	1869–1877
19.	Rutherford Birchard Hayes	1877–1881
20.	James A. Garfield	1881
21.	Chester Alan Arthur	1881–1885
22.	Grover Cleveland	1885–1889
23.	Benjamin Harrison	1889–1893
24.	Grover Cleveland	1893–1897
25.	William McKinley	1897–1901

26.	Theodore Roosevelt	1901–1909
27.	William Howard Taft	1909–1913
28.	Woodrow Wilson	1913–1921
29.	Warren Gamaliel Harding	1921–1923
30.	Calvin Coolidge	1923–1929
31.	Herbert Clark Hoover	1929–1933
32.	Franklin Delano Roosevelt	1933–1945
33.	Harry S. Truman	1945–1953
34.	Dwight David Eisenhower	1953–1961
35.	John Fitzgerald Kennedy	1961–1963
36.	Lyndon Baines Johnson	1963–1969
37.	Richard Milhous Nixon	1969–1974
38.	Gerald Rudolph Ford (appointed)	1974–1977
39.	James Earl Carter	1977–1981
40.	Ronald Wilson Reagan	1981–

26.	Theodore Roosevelt	1901–1909
27.	William Howard Taft	1909–1913
28.	Woodrow Wilson	1913–1921
29.	Warren Gamaliel Harding	1921–1923
30.	Calvin Coolidge	1923–1929
31.	Herbert Clark Hoover	1929–1933
32.	Franklin Delano Roosevelt	1933–1945
33.	Harry S. Truman	1945–1953
34.	Dwight David Eisenhower	1953–1961
35.	John Fitzgerald Kennedy	1961–1963
36.	Lyndon Baines Johnson	1963–1969
37.	Richard Milhous Nixon	1969–1974
38.	Gerald R. Ford (designado)	1974–1977
39.	James Earl Carter	1977–1981
40.	Ronald Wilson Reagan	1981–

American Government

Questions and Answers

1. *Q.* How does the Government get the money needed to carry on its affairs?
   A. By taxation.

2. *Q.* Who levies the taxes?
   A. Congress.

3. *Q.* Where is the original document of the Constitution located?
   A. In the National Archives, in Washington, D.C.

4. *Q.* Do you know the names of the first three Presidents?
   A. Yes: George Washington, John Adams, and Thomas Jefferson.

5. *Q.* Who wrote the pledge to the flag of the United States (Pledge of Allegiance)?
   A. Francis Bellamy.

6. *Q.* Who elects the President?
   A. The people, through the Electoral College.

7. *Q.* In what state are you now living?
   A. In —— *(give the name of your state).*

El Sistema Americano de Gobierno

Preguntas y Respuestas

1. *P.* ¿Cómo el Gobierno consigue el dinero que necesita para poder ejercer sus funciones?
   R. Mediante la imposición de tributos o impuestos.

2. *P.* ¿Quién exige los impuestos?
   R. El Congreso.

3. *P.* ¿Dónde se conserva el original de la Constitución?
   R. En el Archivo Nacional, en Washington, D.C.

4. *P.* ¿Sabe usted los nombres de los primeros tres Presidentes?
   R. Sí: George Washington, John Adams y Thomas Jefferson.

5. *P.* ¿Quién escribió la Promesa de Fidelidad a la bandera americana?
   R. Francis Bellamy.

6. *P.* ¿Quién elije al Presidente?
   R. El pueblo, a través de los *compromisarios.* (El pueblo de cada Estado vota por un "colegio electoral" compuesto de tantos compromisarios o electores como Senadores y Representantes tiene el Estado en el Congreso (otros tres son electos por el Distrito de Columbia) y estos compromisarios eligen al Presidente. Así, pues, la elección del Presidente por el pueblo es indirecta.)

7. *P.* ¿En qué Estado vive usted actualmente?
   R. En ——— *(Dé el nombre de su Estado).*

8. *Q.* Who makes the laws in your state?
   A. The State Legislature.

9. *Q.* Did we have a government before the Constitution?
   A. Yes, we had a government under the Articles of Confederation.

10. *Q.* What is the 22nd Amendment?
    A. The president can serve only 2 terms.

11. *Q.* What are the divisions of Congress?
    A. The Senate and the House of Representatives.

12. *Q.* What body advises the President in making policy decisions?
    A. A cabinet made up of 11 members.

13. *Q.* Can the President make treaties with other nations?
    A. Yes, he can make treaties with the consent of the Senate.

14. *Q.* What is the 26th Amendment?
    A. That a person 18 years of age or older can vote.

15. *Q.* What do you pledge when you stand before the national flag?
    A. *I pledge allegiance to the flag of the United States of America, and to the Republic for which it stands; one nation under God, indivisible, with liberty and justice for all.*

16. *Q.* How does an amendment become part of the Constitution?
    A. It is passed by Congress with a two-thirds vote and by a three-fourths vote in the State Legislatures.

8. *P.* ¿Quién crea las leyes en su Estado?
   R. La Legislatura Estatal.

9. *P.* ¿Teníamos un gobierno antes de que fuera aprobada la Constitución?
   R. Sí, teníamos un gobierno regido por los Artículos de Confederación.

10. *P.* ¿Qué dispone la Vigésimasegunda (22da) Enmienda?
    R. Que el Presidente sólo puede servir dos períodos.

11. *P.* ¿Cuáles son los dos cuerpos legislativos que componen el Congreso?
    R. El Senado y la Cámara de Representantes.

12. *P.* ¿Qué organismo asesora al Presidente con respecto a las decisiones de carácter político?
    R. El Gabinete, que se compone de 11 ministros, llamados *Secretarios.*

13. *P.* ¿Puede el Presidente negociar tratados con otras naciones?
    R. Sí, con el consentimiento del Senado.

14. *P.* ¿Qué dispone la Vigésimasexta (26ta) Enmienda?
    R. Que para poder votar un ciudadano tiene que tener no menos de 18 años de edad.

15. *P.* ¿A qué se compromete usted cuando se pone de pie ante la bandera nacional y repite la Promesa de Fidelidad?
    R. *Declaro fidelidad a la Bandera de Estados Unidos de América y a la República que representa, una nación bajo Dios, indivisible, con libertad y justicia para todos.*

16. *P.* ¿Cómo una Enmienda se convierte en parte de la Constitución?
    R. Siendo aprobada en el Congreso por una mayoría de dos tercios (2/3), y por una mayoría de tres cuartas partes (3/4) en las Legislaturas Estatales.

17. *Q.* What is your nationality?
    A. *(Give correct answer.)*

18. *Q.* In order, name the successors to the President in case the President resigns or dies.
    A. 1. The Vice President
    2. The Speaker of the House.
    3. The President *pro tempore* of the Senate.

19. *Q.* What does impeachment mean?
    A. It means officially accusing an officer of wrongdoing and forcing that official to resign.

20. *Q.* How long does a Federal judge serve?
    A. For life, unless he or she is charged with unbecoming conduct.

21. *Q.* What is the 20th Amendment?
    A. It changed the date of the President's inauguration to January 20 and the opening date of Congress to January 3.

22. *Q.* (a) What is the Legislative Branch of the United States government?
    A. The Congress.
    Q. (b) What is the Executive Branch?
    A. The President and his Cabinet.
    Q. (c) What is the Judicial Branch?
    A. The courts.

23. *Q.* Can Congress pass a bill in spite of the President's veto?
    A. Yes, by a two-thirds majority of Congress.

17. *P.* ¿Cuál es su nacionalidad?
R. *(Dé la respuesta correcta.)*

18. *P.* Nombre en el orden debido a los sucesores del Presidente, en caso de que éste renuncie o muera.
R. 1. El Vice Presidente.
2. El Presidente ("Speaker") de la Cámara.
3. El Presidente *pro tempore* del Senado. ("Pro tempore", es decir, quien está actuando *temporalmente* como presidente, en ausencia del presidente en propiedad.)

19. *P.* ¿Qué significa el proceso de *residenciar* a un funcionario público? ("Impeachment")
R. Significa acusarlo de conducta impropia o criminal en el desempeño de su cargo; y, de ser encontrado culpable, obligarlo a renunciar.

20. *P.* ¿Por cuántos años son nombrados los jueces Federales?
R. El nombramiento es vitalicio, excepto en el caso de un magistrado que sea acusado y convicto de conducta impropia o criminal.

21. *P.* ¿Qué dispuso la Vigésima (20ma) Enmienda?
R. Cambió la fecha de la toma de posesión del Presidente para el 20 de enero después de su elección, y la del comienzo de las sesiones del Congreso, para el día 3 de ese mismo mes.

22. *P.* (*a*) ¿Cuál es la Rama Ejecutiva del gobierno de los Estados Unidos?
R. El Presidente y su Gabinete.

P. (*b*) ¿Cuál es la Rama Legislativa?
R. El Congreso.

23. *P.* ¿Puede el Congreso aprobar un *proyecto de ley* ("bill") a pesar del *veto* (oposición) del Presidente?
R. Sí, por una mayoría congresional de dos terceras partes (2/3) de los votos emitidos.

24. *Q.* Who appoints the justices of the Supreme Court?
    A. The President, with the consent of the Senate.

25. *Q.* What are the qualifications for Vice President?
    A. The same as for the President.

26. *Q.* What are the principles of the United States Constitution?
    A. Liberty, equality, and justice.

27. *Q.* What are the first 10 Amendments called?
    A. The Bill of Rights.

28. *Q.* What is a democratic government?
    A. Government by the people through their elected representatives.

29. *Q.* What are the qualifications for United States Senator?
    A. A Senator must be an American citizen, 30 years old or more. He or she must have lived in the United States for more than nine (9) years as an American citizen.

30. *Q.* What are the qualifications for United States Representative (Congressman)?
    A. A Representative must be an American citizen, 25 years old or more, who has lived in the United States for more than seven (7) years as an American citizen.

31. *Q.* What is meant by a Presidential veto?
    A. It is the President's refusal to sign a bill which has been passed by Congress.

32. *Q.* Is the American government a federation or centralized?
    A. It is a federation.

24. *P.* ¿Quién nombra los jueces de la Corte Suprema?
R. El Presidente, con la aprobación del Senado.

25. *P.* ¿Cuáles son las calificaciones para el Vice Presidente?
R. Las mismas que para el Presidente.

26. *P.* ¿Cuáles son los principios fundamentales de la Constitución de los Estados Unidos?
R. Libertad, igualdad y justicia.

27. *P.* ¿Cómo se le llama a las 10 primeras Enmiendas?
R. La Carta de Derechos.

28. *P.* ¿Qué es un gobierno democrático?
R. Un gobierno del pueblo, ejercido a través de sus representantes libremente electos.

29. *P.* ¿Cuáles son las calificaciones para un Senador Federal?
R. Un Senador debe ser mayor de 30 años de edad y ciudadano americano. Debe haber residido en los Estados Unidos, como ciudadano, por lo menos durante 9 años antes de su elección.

30. *P.* ¿Cuáles son las calificaciones para un Representante Federal? (Congresista)
R. Un Representante debe ser mayor de 25 años de edad y ciudadano americano. Debe haber residido en Estados Unidos, como ciudadano, por lo menos durante 7 años antes de su elección.

31. *P.* ¿Qué significa el *veto* presidencial?
R. La negativa del Presidente a firmar un *proyecto de ley* ("bill") que ha sido aprobado por el Congreso.

32. *P.* ¿Qué tipo de gobierno establece la Constitución, centralista o federado?
R. Federado.

33. *Q.* Who makes the laws for each of the 50 states?
A. The state legislature of each state.

34. *Q.* Who is the head of the Supreme Court?
A. The Chief Justice.

35. *Q.* What are the major political parties in the United States?
A. The Democratic party and the Republican party.

36. *Q.* Has any President been impeached?
A. Yes. Andrew Johnson was impeached in 1868, but he was not convicted.

37. *Q.* Who is the head of the Armed Forces?
A. The President.

38. *Q.* Can the President declare war?
A. No.

39. *Q.* Can any state make a treaty or alliance with a foreign country?
A. No, only the Federal Government can do so.

40. *Q.* What is the 16th Amendment?
A. It allows the government to tax incomes.

41. *Q.* What is the 19th Amendment?
A. It gives women the right to vote.

42. *Q.* How many Senators are there in Congress?
A. There are 100.

33. *P.* ¿Quién crea las leyes para cada uno de los 50 Estados?
R. La Legislatura Estatal de cada Estado.

34. *P.* ¿Quién es el jefe de la Corte Suprema?
R. El Juez Presidente.

35. *P.* ¿Cuáles son los principales partidos políticos en los Estados Unidos?
R. El Partido Demócrata y el Partido Republicano.

36. *P.* ¿Ha sido alguna vez *residenciado* ("impeached") un Presidente? (Esto es, acusado de conducta impropia o criminal ante un tribunal competente.)
R. Sí. Andrew Johnson fue *residenciado* en 1868, pero no fue convicto.

37. *P.* ¿Quién es el Comandante-en-Jefe de las Fuerzas Armadas?
R. El Presidente.

38. *P.* ¿Tiene poderes el Presidente para declarar la guerra?
R. No. La declara el Congreso.

39. *P.* ¿Puede algún Estado negociar un tratado o alianza con un gobierno extranjero?
R. No, eso sólo puede hacerlo el Gobierno Federal.

40. *P.* ¿Qué dispone la Décimosexta (16ta) Enmienda?
R. Que el gobierno puede imponer tributos sobre los ingresos.

41. *P.* ¿Qué dispone la Décimonona (19na) Enmienda?
R. Que las mujeres tienen derecho al voto.

42. *P.* ¿Cuántos Senadores hay en el Congreso?
R. Hay 100 Senadores.

43. *Q.* How many Amendments are there to the United States Constitution?
    A. There are 26 Amendments.

44. *Q.* What are the qualifications for President?
    A. The President must be over 35 years of age and a native-born citizen, who has lived in the United States for more than 14 years.

45. *Q.* Is the United States a dictatorship, a monarchy, or a republic?
    A. The United States is a republic.

46. *Q.* How many Representatives does each state have?
    A. The number depends on the population of each state.

47. *Q.* How many Senators does each state have?
    A. Each state has two (2) Senators.

48. *Q.* Who is the President of the United States at present?
    A. *(Give correct name of person now holding office.)*

49. *Q.* Who is the Vice President of the United States?
    A. *(Give correct name of person now holding office.)*

50. *Q.* Do you know the current population of the United States?
    A. Around 226 million.

51. *Q.* How long is a term in office for the President?
    A. Four years.

43. *P.* ¿Cuántas Enmiendas se le han hecho a la Constitución?
R. Veintiséis (26) Enmiendas.

44. *P.* ¿Cuáles son las calificaciones para Presidente?
R. El Presidente tiene que ser ciudadano americano por nacimiento, y mayor de 35 años de edad. Debe haber residido en los Estados Unidos durante más de 14 años antes de su elección.

45. *P.* ¿Qué es los Estados Unidos, una dictadura, una monarquía o una república?
R. Los Estados Unidos es una república.

46. *P.* ¿Cuántos Representantes (Congresistas) tiene cada Estado?
R. El número depende de la población que tenga cada Estado.

47. *P.* ¿Cuántos Senadores tiene cada Estado?
R. Cada Estado tiene dos (2) Senadores.

48. *P.* ¿Quién es actualmente el Presidente de los Estados Unidos?
R. *(Dé el nombre correcto de la persona que esté actualmente desempeñando dicho cargo.)*

49. *P.* ¿Quién es el Vice Presidente de los Estados Unidos?
R. *(Dé el nombre correcto de la persona que esté actualmente desempeñando dicho cargo.)*

50. *P.* ¿Sabe usted a cuántos habitantes asciende actualmente la población de los Estados Unidos?
R. Alrededor de 226 millones.

51. *P.* ¿De cuántos años es un período en el cargo de Presidente?
R. Cuatro años.

52. *Q.* How long is the term for a Senator?
A. Six years.

53. *Q.* How long is the term for a Representative?
A. Two years.

54. *Q.* What is an Amendment?
A. It is a change or an addition to the Constitution.

55. *Q.* Who makes the laws of the United States?
A. The Congress.

56. *Q.* If the President dies or cannot perform his duties, who takes his place?
A. The Vice President.

57. *Q.* What are the three United States courts?
A. 1. The United States Supreme Court.
2. The United States Circuit Court.
3. The United States District Court.

58. *Q.* What is the highest court in the United States?
A. It is the United States Supreme Court.

59. *Q.* How many justices are there in the United States Supreme Court?
A. There are nine justices.

60. *Q.* What are the three branches of the United States government?
A. 1. Legislative.
2. Executive.
3. Judicial.

61. *Q.* How are the State Representatives selected?
A. They are elected by registered voters within each state.

52. *P.* ¿De cuántos años es un período en el cargo de Senador?
R. Seis años.

53. *P.* ¿De cuántos años es un período en el cargo de Representante?
R. Dos años.

54. *P.* ¿Qué es una Enmienda?
R. Es un cambio o añadidura a la Constitución.

55. *P.* ¿Quién crea las leyes de los Estados Unidos?
R. El Congreso.

56. *P.* Si el Presidente muere o queda incapacitado para desempeñar los deberes de su cargo, ¿quién lo substituye?
R. El Vice Presidente.

57. *P.* ¿Cuáles son las tres Cortes Federales?
R. 1. La Corte Suprema de los Estados Unidos.
2. La Corte de Circuito de los Estados Unidos.
3. La Corte de Distrito de los Estados Unidos.

58. *P.* ¿Cuál es el tribunal más alto de los Estados Unidos?
R. La Corte Suprema de los Estados Unidos.

59. *P.* ¿Cuántos jueces integran la Corte Suprema de los Estados Unidos?
R. Nueve magistrados; el Juez Presidente y 8 Jueces Asociados.

60. *P.* ¿Cuáles son las tres ramas del Gobierno Federal?
R. 1. Ejecutiva.
2. Legislativa.
3. Judicial.

61. *P.* ¿Cómo son seleccionados los Representantes Estatales?
R. Son electos por los votantes inscritos ("registered") en cada Estado.

62. *Q.* Who is the Governor of your state?
A. *(Give correct name of person now holding office.)*

63. *Q.* Name one Congressman and one Senator from your state.
A. *(Give correct names of the people holding these offices.)*

64. *Q.* When was your state admitted to the Union?
A. *(Give correct date for the state in which you live.)*

65. *Q.* Where is the United States Supreme Court located?
A. In Washington, D.C.

66. *Q.* What is the Cabinet?
A. It is a group of people selected by the President and approved by the Senate who assist the President in special areas such as agriculture, commerce, foreign affairs, etc.

67. *Q.* Do you know the name of the bird that is the symbol of the United States?
A. Yes, the bald eagle.

68. *Q.* What were the Articles of Confederation?
A. They were the first Constitution of the United States.

69. *Q.* Who is Chief Executive of the United States?
A. The President.

70. *Q.* Who said the following famous words? "Government of the people, by the people, for the people."
A. Abraham Lincoln, in the Gettysburg Address (1863).

62. *P.* ¿Quién es el Gobernador de su Estado?
R. *(Dé el nombre correcto de la persona que esté actualmente desempeñando dicho cargo.)*

63. *P.* Nombre un Congresista y un Senador Federal que estén representando a su Estado en Washington.
R. *(Dé los nombres correctos de dos personas que estén actualmente desempeñando dichos cargos.)*

64. *P.* ¿En qué año fue su Estado admitido a la Unión?
R. *(Dé la fecha correcta que corresponde al Estado en que usted vive.)*

65. *P.* ¿Dónde está situada la Corte Suprema de los Estados Unidos?
R. En Washington, D.C.

66. *P.* ¿Qué es el Gabinete Ejecutivo?
R. Es un grupo de 11 ministros seleccionados por el Presidente, con la aprobación del Senado. Se les conoce como *Secretarios* y su labor consiste en asesorar al Primer Mandatario en varios campos de especial importancia, tales como la agricultura, el comercio, las relaciones internacionales, etc.

67. *P.* ¿Sabe usted cuál es el ave que es el símbolo de los Estados Unidos?
R. Sí, el águila calva americana.

68. *P.* ¿Qué eran los Artículos de Confederación?
R. La primera Constitución de los Estados Unidos.

69. *P.* ¿Quién es el Primer Ejecutivo de los Estados Unidos?
R. El Presidente.

70. *P.* Las palabras que vamos a citar a continuación son famosas, ¿quién las pronunció? "Un gobierno del pueblo, por el pueblo y para el pueblo."
R. Abraham Lincoln, en su Discurso de Gettysburg, pronunciado en 1863.

71. *Q.* Why were the Articles of Confederation discarded in favor of the present Constitution?
    A. Because Congress could make laws but could not enforce them, and there was no unity among the states.

72. *Q.* Can the residents of Washington, D.C., vote?
    A. Yes, in Federal elections and for mayor.

73. *Q.* What United States officials are elected by the people?
    A. The President, Vice President, Senators, and Representatives.

74. *Q.* Why do you want to become an American citizen?
    A. 1. *Example:* Because I am married to a person who is an American citizen.
    2. *Example:* Because I like the freedom and democracy of the United States.

71. *P.* ¿Por qué fueron descartados los Artículos de Confederación y substituídos con la actual Constitución?
R. Porque el Congreso no podía poner en vigor las leyes que aprobaba, y no había unidad entre los Estados.

72. *P.* ¿Pueden votar los residentes del Distrito de Columbia, en Washington?
R. Sí, en las elecciones nacionales, y también para elegir al alcalde.

73. *P.* ¿Cuáles funcionarios Federales son electos por el pueblo?
R. El Presidente, el Vice Presidente, los Senadores y los Representantes (Congresistas).

74. *P.* ¿Por qué quiere usted adquirir la ciudadanía americana?
R. 1. *Ejemplo:* Porque mi cónyuge es ciudadano americano.
2. *Ejemplo:* Porque me agrada la libertad y la democracia que se disfruta en los Estados Unidos.

General Information

Sample Sentences

Write the following sentences, completing those which have blanks for answer choices.

1. I want to be an American citizen.
2. I have studied the American Constitution.
3. I have a pen in my right hand.
4. Today is a beautiful day.
5. This pen has———*(blue, black)* ink.
6. I went to a citizenship school for two months.
7. There are three colors in our flag: red, white, and blue.
8. There are fifty (50) states in the United States.
9. I came to———*(state)* from———*(country)* on———*(April 5th) (yesterday) (last week)*.
10. I am wearing a———*(blue, red, green)* dress.
11. I am here to take my test today.
12. Yesterday was a———*(cold, warm, hot)* day.
13. I can read, write, and speak simple English.
14. There are many cars on the street.

Información General

Ejemplos de Oraciones Sencillas

Estudie las siguientes oraciones y luego escríbalas en inglés, según aparecen en la página opuesta, y complete aquéllas que tengan espacios en blanco para escoger las respuestas. (La numeración de las oraciones en ambas páginas es idéntica.)

1. Yo quiero ser ciudadano americano.
2. Yo he estudiado la Constitución americana.
3. Yo tengo una pluma en mi mano derecha.
4. Hoy es un día bello.
5. Esta pluma tiene tinta————*(azul, negra)*.
6. Yo asistí durante dos meses a una escuela donde dictaban clases sobre ciudadanía.
7. Nuestra bandera tiene tres colores: rojo, blanco y azul.
8. En los Estados Unidos hay cincuenta (50) Estados.
9. Yo vine a————*(Estado)* de————*(país)* el ————*(5 de abril) (ayer) (la semana pasada)*.
10. Yo tengo puesto un traje————*(azul, rojo, verde)*.
11. Yo he venido aquí para tomar hoy mi prueba.
12. Ayer fue un día————*(frío, cálido, canicular)*.
13. Yo puedo leer, escribir y hablar inglés elemental.
14. Hay muchos carros en la calle.

15. I am working at———.

16. I am wearing———*(yellow, brown, gray)* shoes.

17. It is raining now.

18. I have been married for———years.

19. We do not have any children (yet).

20. We have———children:———sons and———daughters.

21. We have———son (s).

22. My first name is———.

23. I was married———years ago.

24. May I write something else?

25. I will do my best to be a worthy citizen.

26. I enjoy my work.

15. Yo estoy trabajando en————.

16. Yo tengo puestos zapatos————*(amarillos, pardos, grises)*.

17. Ahora está lloviendo.

18. Yo llevo————años de casado (a).

19. Nosotros no tenemos hijos (todavía).

20. Nosotros tenemos————niños:————hijos y ————hijas.

21. Nosotros tenemos————hijo (s).

22. Mi primer nombre es————.

23. Hace————años que yo estoy casado (a).

24. ¿Podría escribir otra cosa?

25. Yo haré todo lo posible por ser un ciudadano honorable.

26. Yo estoy a gusto en mi trabajo.

Servicio de Inmigración y Naturalización

Oficinas de Distrito

Alaska
U.S. Post Office & Courthouse
Building, Room 143
Anchorage, Alaska 99501

Arizona
230 North First Avenue
Phoenix, Arizona 85025

California
300 North Los Angeles Street
Los Angeles, California 90012

Appraisers Building
630 Sansome Street
San Francisco, California 94111

Colorado
17027 Federal Office Building
Denver, Colorado 80202

Connecticut
135 High Street
P.O. Box 1724
Hartford, Connecticut 06101

Florida
Room 1402, Federal Building
51 S.W. First Avenue
Miami, Florida 33130

Georgia
881 Peachtree Street, N.E.
Atlanta, Georgia 30309

Hawaii
595 Ala Moana Boulevard
P.O. Box 461
Honolulu, Hawaii 96809

Illinois
Courthouse & Federal Office Building
219 South Dearborn Street
Chicago, Illinois 60604

Louisiana
New Federal Building
701 Loyola Avenue
New Orleans, Louisiana 70113

Maine
319 U.S. Courthouse
P.O. Box 578
Portland, Maine 04112

Maryland
707 North Calvert Street
Baltimore, Maryland 21202

Massachusetts
150 Tremont Street
Boston, Massachusetts 02111

Michigan
Federal Building
333 Mount Elliott Street
Detroit, Michigan 48207

Minnesota
1014 New Post Office Building
180 E. Kellogg Boulevard
St. Paul, Minnesota 55101

Missouri
819 U.S. Courthouse
811 Grand Avenue
Kansas City, Missouri 64106

Montana
Federal Building
P.O. Box 1724
Helena, Montana 59601

Nebraska
New Federal Building
215 North 17th Street
Omaha, Nebraska 68102

New Jersey
1060 Broad Street
Newark, New Jersey 07102

New York
68 Court Street
Buffalo, New York 14202

20 West Broadway
New York, New York 10007

Ohio
600 Standard Building
1370 Ontario Street
Cleveland, Ohio 44113

Oregon
333 U.S. Courthouse
Broadway & Main Streets
Portland, Oregon 97205

Pennsylvania
128 North Broad Street
Philadelphia, Pennsylvania 19102

Texas
343 U.S. Courthouse
P.O. Box 9398
El Paso, Texas 79984

Route 3
Los Fresnos, Texas 78566

U.S. Post Office & Courthouse
P.O. Box 2539
San Antonio, Texas 78206

Vermont
45 Kingman Street
St. Albans, Vermont 05478

Washington, D.C.
1025 Vermont Avenue, N.W.
Washington, D.C. 20536

Washington
815 Airport Way, S.
Seattle, Washington 98134

Puerto Rico
804 Ponce de Leon Avenue
Santurce
San Juan, Puerto Rico 00908

The Declaration of Independence

In Congress, July 4, 1776

The Unanimous Declaration of the Thirteen United States of America

When in the course of human events, it becomes necessary for one people to dissolve the political bands which have connected them with another, and to assume among the powers of the earth, the separate and equal station to which the laws of Nature and of Nature's God entitle them, a decent respect to the opinions of mankind requires that they should declare the causes which impel them to the separation.

We hold these truths to be self-evident, that all men are created equal, that they are endowed by their Creator with certain unalienable rights, that among these are life, liberty and the pursuit of happiness. That to secure these rights, governments are instituted among men, deriving their just powers from the consent of the governed,—That whenever any form of government becomes destructive of these ends, it is the right of the people to alter or to abolish it, and to institute new government, laying its foundation on such principles and organizing its powers in such form, as to them shall seem most likely to effect their safety and happiness. Prudence, indeed, will dictate that governments long established should not be changed for light and transient causes; and accordingly all experience hath shown, that man-kind are more disposed to suffer, while evils are sufferable, than to right themselves by abolishing the forms to which they are accustomed. But when a long train of abuses and usurpations, pursuing invariably the same object evinces a design to reduce them under absolute despotism, it is their right, it is their duty, to throw off such government, and to provide new guards for their future security.—Such has been the patient sufferance of these Colonies; and such is now the necessity which constrains them to alter their former systems of government. The history of the present King of Great Britain is a history of repeated injuries and usurpations, all having in direct object the establishment of an absolute tyranny over these States. To prove this, let facts be submitted to a candid world.

He has refused his assent to laws, the most wholesome and necessary for the public good.

He has forbidden his Governors to pass laws of immediate and pressing importance, unless suspended in their operation till his assent should be obtained; and when so suspended, he has utterly neglected to attend to them.

He has refused to pass other laws for the accommodation of large districts of people, unless those people would relinquish the right of representation in the legislature, a right inestimable to them and formidable to tyrants only.

He has called together legislative bodies at places unusual, uncomfortable, and distant from the depository of their public records, for the sole purpose of fatiguing them into compliance with his measures.

He has dissolved Representative Houses repeatedly, for opposing with manly firmness his invasions on the rights of the people.

He has refused for a long time, after such dissolutions, to cause others to be elected; whereby the legislative powers, incapable of annihilation, have returned to the people at large for their exercise; the State remaining in the mean time exposed to all the dangers of invasion from without, and convulsions within.

He has endeavoured to prevent the population of these States; for that purpose obstructing the laws for naturalization of foreigners; refusing to pass others to encourage their migrations hither, and raising the conditions of new appropriations of lands.

He has obstructed the administration of justice, by refusing his assent to laws for establishing judiciary powers.

He has made judges dependent on his will alone, for the

tenure of their offices, and the amount and payment of their salaries.

He has erected a multitude of new offices, and sent hither swarms of officers to harass our people, and eat out their substance.

He has kept among us, in times of peace, standing armies without the consent of our legislatures.

He has affected to render the military independent of and superior to the civil power.

He has combined with others to subject us to a jurisdiction foreign to our constitution, and unacknowledged by our laws; giving his assent to their acts of pretended legislation:

For quartering large bodies of armed troops among us:

For protecting them, by a mock trial, from punishment for any murders which they should commit on the inhabitants of these States:

For cutting off our trade with all parts of the world:

For imposing taxes on us without our consent:

For depriving us in many cases, of the benefits of trial by jury:

For transporting us beyond seas to be tried for pretended offenses:

For abolishing the free system of English laws in a neighbouring province, establishing therein an arbitrary government, and enlarging its boundaries so as to render it at once an example and fit instrument for introducing the same absolute rule into these colonies:

For taking away our charters, abolishing our most valuable laws, and altering fundamentally the forms of our governments:

For suspending our own legislatures, and declaring themselves invested with power to legislate for us in all cases whatsoever.

He has abdicated government here, by declaring us out of his protection and waging war against us.

He has plundered our seas, ravaged our coasts, burnt our towns, and destroyed the lives of our people.

He is at this time transporting large armies of foreign mercenaries to complete the works of death, desolation and tyranny, already begun with circumstances of cruelty and perfidy scarcely paralleled in the most barbarous ages, and totally unworthy the head of a civilized nation.

He has constrained our fellow citizens taken captive on the high seas to bear arms against their country, to become the executioners of their friends and brethren, or to fall themselves by their hands.

He has excited domestic insurrections amongst us, and has endeavoured to bring on the inhabitants of our frontiers, the merciless Indian savages, whose known rule of warfare is an undistinguished destruction of all ages, sexes and conditions.

In every stage of these oppressions we have petitioned for redress in the most humble terms: Our repeated petitions have been answered only by repeated injury. A prince, whose character is thus marked by every act which may define a tyrant, is unfit to be the ruler of a free people.

Nor have we been wanting in attentions to our British brethren. We have warned them from time to time of attempts by their legislature to extend an unwarrantable jurisdiction over us. We have reminded them of the circumstances of our emigration and settlement here. We have appealed to their native justice and magnanimity, and we have conjured them by the ties of our common kindred to disavow these usurpations, which, would inevitably interrupt our connections and correspondence. They too have been deaf to the voice of justice and of consanguinity. We must, therefore, acquiesce in the necessity which denounces our separation, and hold them, as we hold the rest of mankind, enemies in war, in peace friends.

WE, THEREFORE, the Representatives of the United States of America, in General Congress, Assembled, appealing to the Supreme Judge of the world for the rectitude of our intentions, do, in the name, and by authority of the good people of these Colonies, solemnly publish and declare, That these United Colonies are, and of right ought to be FREE AND INDEPENDENT STATES; that they are absolved from all allegiance to the British Crown, and that all political connection between them and the State of Great Britain, is and ought to be totally dissolved; and that as free and independent States, they have full power to levy war, conclude peace, contract alliances, establish commerce, and to do all other acts and things which independent States may of right do. And for the support of this Declaration, with a firm reliance on the protection of Divine Providence, we mutually pledge to each other our lives, our fortunes and our sacred honor.

John Hancock.

New Hampshire

Josiah Bartlett
Wm. Whipple
Matthew Thornton

Massachusetts Bay

Saml. Adams
John Adams
Robt. Treat Paine
Elbridge Gerry

Rhode Island

Step. Hopkins
William Ellery

Connecticut

Roger Sherman
Saml. Huntington
Wm. Williams
Oliver Wolcott

New York

Wm. Floyd
Phil. Livingston
Frans. Lewis
Lewis Morris

New Jersey

Richd. Stockton
Jno. Witherspoon
Fras. Hopkinson
John Hart
Abra. Clark

Pennsylvania

Robt. Morris
Benjamin Rush
Jas. Smith
Geo. Taylor

Benja. Franklin
John Morton
Geo. Clymer
James Wilson
Geo. Ross

Delaware

Caesar Rodney
Geo. Read
Tho. M'Kean

Maryland

Samuel Chase
Wm. Paca
Thos. Stone
Charles Carroll
of Carrollton

Virginia

George Wythe
Richard Henry Lee
Th. Jefferson
Benja. Harrison
Thos. Nelson Jr.
Francis Lightfoot Lee
Carter Braxton

North Carolina

Wm. Hooper
Joseph Hewes
John Penn

South Carolina

Edward Rutledge
Thos. Heyward Junr.
Thomas Lynch Junr.
Arthur Middleton

Georgia

Button Gwinnett
Lyman Hall
Geo. Walton

La Declaración de Independencia de los Estados Unidos

La Declaracion de Independencia fue adoptada en Filadelfia, en el 4 de Julio de 1776, por el Congreso Continental.

Cuando, en el curso de los acontecimientos humanos, un pueblo se ve en la necesidad de disolver los lazos políticos que lo han unido con otro, y ocupar, entre las naciones de la tierra, un sitio separado e igual, al cual tiene derecho según las Leyes de la Naturaleza y el Dios de esa Naturaleza; el respeto debido a las opiniones del género humano exige que se declaren las causas que han obligado a ese pueblo a la separación.

Aceptamos como verdades evidentes que todos los hombres nacen iguales, que están dotados por su Creador de ciertos derechos inalienables, entre los cuales están el derecho a la Vida, a la Libertad y al logro de la Felicidad; que, para asegurar estos derechos, los hombres establecen Gobiernos, derivando sus justos poderes del consentimiento de los gobernados; que cuando una forma de gobierno se convierte en destructora de estos fines, es un derecho del pueblo cambiarla o abolirla, e instituir un nuevo gobierno, basado en esos principios y organizando su autoridad en la forma que el pueblo estime como la más conveniente para obtener su seguridad y su felicidad. En realidad, la prudencia recomienda que los gobiernos erigidos mucho tiempo atrás no sean cambiados por causas sencillas y transitorias; en efecto, la experiencia ha demostrado que la humanidad está más bien dispuesta para sufrir, mientras los males sean tolerables que a hacerse justicia aboliendo las formas de gobierno a las cuales se encuentra acostumbrada. Pero cuando una larga cadena de abusos y usurpaciones, que persiguen invariablemente el mismo objetivo, hace patente la intención de reducir al pueblo a un despotismo absoluto, es derecho del hombre, es su obligación, expulsar a ese gobierno y buscar nuevos guardianes para su seguridad futura. Tal ha sido el paciente sufrimiento de estas colonias; tal es ahora la necesidad que las obliga a cambiar sus antiguos sistemas de Gobierno. La historia del actual rey de la Gran Bretaña es una historia de agravios y usurpaciones repetidas, que tienen como meta directa la de establecer una tiranía absoluta en estos Estados. Para demostrar lo anterior presentamos los siguientes hechos ante un mundo que no los conoce:

El Rey ha rehusado a aprobar las leyes más favorables y necesarias para el bienestar público.

Ha prohibido a sus gobernadores aprobar leyes de importancia inmediata y apremiante, a menos que su ejecución se suspenda hasta obtener su aprobación; y, una vez suspendidas, se ha negado por completo a prestarles atención.

Ha rehusado a aprobar otra leyes convenientes a grandes comarcas pobladas, a menos que esos pueblos renuncien al derecho de ser representados en la Legislatura; derecho que es inestimable para el pueblo y perjudicial sólo para los tiranos.

Ha convocado a los cuerpos legislativos en sitios desusados, incómodos y distantes del asiento de sus documentos públicos, con la sola idea de fatigarlos para cumplir con sus medidas.

En repetidas ocasiones ha disuelto las Cámaras de Representantes, por oponerse con firmeza viril a sus intromisiones en los derechos del pueblo.

Durante mucho tiempo, y después de esas disoluciones, ha rehusado permitir la elección de otras cámaras; por lo cual, los poderes legislativos, cuyo aniquilamiento es imposible, han retornado al pueblo, sin limitación para su ejercicio; permaneciendo el Estado, mientras tanto, expuesto a todos los peligros de una invasión exterior y a convulsiones internas.

Ha tratado de impedir que aumente de poblacion estos Estados; entorpeciendo con ese propósito, las Leyes de Naturalización de Extranjeros; rehusando aprobar otras para fomentar su inmigración y elevando las condiciones para las Nuevas Adquisiciones de Tierra.

Ha entorpecido la administración de justicia al no aprobar las leyes que establecen los poderes judiciales.

Ha hecho que los jueces dependan solamente de su voluntad, para poder desempeñar sus cargos y en cuanto a la cantidad y pago de sus emolumentos.

Ha fundado una gran diversidad de nuevas oficinas, enviando a un contingente de funcionarios que acosan a nuestro pueblo y reducen su sustento.

En tiempo de paz, ha mantenido entre nosotros ejércitos permanentes, sin el consentimiento de nuestras legislaturas.

Ha influido para que la autoridad militar sea independiente de la civil y superior a ella.

Se ha asociado con otros para someternos a una jurisdicción extraña a nuestra constitución y no reconocida por nuestras leyes; aprobando sus actos de pretendida legislación:

Para acuartelar, entre nosotros, grandes cuerpos de tropas armadas.

Para protegerlos, por medio de un juicio ficticio, del castigo por los asesinatos que pudieran cometer entre los habitantes de estos Estados.

Para suspender nuestro comercio con todo el mundo.

Para imponernos impuestos sin nuestro consentimiento.

Para privarnos, en muchos casos, de los beneficios de un juicio por jurado.

Para transportarnos más allá de los mares, con el fin de ser juzgados por supuestos agravios.

Para abolir en una provincia vecina el libre sistema de las leyes inglesas, estableciendo en ella un gobierno arbitrario y extendiendo sus límites, con el objeto de dar un ejemplo y disponer de un instrumento adecuado para introducir el mismo gobierno absoluto en estas Colonias.

Para suprimir nuestras Cartas Constitutivas, abolir nuestras leyes más valiosas y alterar en su esencia las formas de nuestros gobiernos.

Para suspender nuestras propias legislaturas y declarase investido con facultades para legislarnos en todos los casos, cualesquiera que éstos sean.

Ha abdicado de su gobierno en estos territorios al declarar

que estamos fuera de su protección y al emprender una guerra contra nosotros.

Ha saqueado nuestros mares, destruido nuestras costas, incendiado nuestros ciudades y arruinado la vida de nuestro pueblo.

Al presente, está transportando grandes ejércitos de extranjeros mercenarios para completar la obra de muerte, desolación y tiranía, ya iniciada en circunstancias de crueldad y perfidia que apenas si encuentran paralelo en las épocas más bárbaras, y por completo indignas del Jefe de una Nación civilizada.

Ha obligado a nuestros ciudadanos, aprehendidos en alta mar, a que tomen armas contra su país, convirtiéndolos así en los verdugos de sus amigos y hermanos, o a morir bajo sus manos.

Ha provocado insurrecciones intestinas entre nosotros y se ha esforzado por lanzar sobre los habitantes de nuestras fronteras a los inmisericordes indios salvajes, cuya conocida disposición para la guerra se distingue por la destrucción de vidas, sin considerar edades, sexos ni condiciones.

En varias oportunidades, hemos pedido una reparación en los términos más humildes; nuestras súplicas constantes han sido contestadas solamente con ofensas repetidas. Un príncipe, cuyo carácter está marcado, en consecuencia, por todas las acciones que definen a un tirano, no es el adecuado para gobernar a un pueblo libre.

Tampoco hemos incurrido en faltas de atención para con nuestros hermanos británicos. Les hemos comunicado, oportunamente, de los esfuerzos de su legislatura para extender una autoridad injustificable sobre nosotros. Les hemos recordado las circunstancias de nuestra emigración y colonización en estos territorios. Hemos apelado a su justicia y magnanimidad naturales, y los hemos conjurado, por los lazos de nuestra común ascendencia, a que repudien esas usurpaciones, las cuales, inevitablemente, llegarían a interrumpir nuestros nexos y correspondencia. Ellos también se han mostrado sordos a la voz de la justicia y de la consanguinidad. Por tanto, aceptamos la necesidad que proclama nuestra separación, y en adelante los consideramos como al resto de la humanidad: Enemigos en la Guerra, Amigos en la Paz.

En consequencia, nosotros, los representantes de los Estados Unidos de América, reunidos en Congreso General, y apelando al Juez Supremo del Mundo en cuanto a la rectitud de nuestras intenciones, en el nombre, y por la autoridad del buen pueblo de estas Colonias, solemnemente publicamos y declaramos, que estas Colonias Unidas son, y de derecho deben ser, Estados Libres e Independientes; que se hallan exentos de toda fidelidad a la Corona Británica, y que todos los lazos políticos entre ellos y el Estado de la Gran Bretaña son y deben ser totalmente disueltos; y que, como Estados Libres e Independientes, tienen poderes suficientes para declarar la guerra, concertar la paz, celebrar alianzas, establecer el comercio y para efectuar todos aquellos actos y cosas que los Estados Independientes pueden, por su derecho, llevar a cabo.

Y, en apoyo de esta declaración, confiando firmemente en la protección de la Divina Providencia, comprometemos mutuamente nuestras vidas, nuestros bienes y nuestro honor sacrosanto.

John Hancock.

New Hampshire

Josiah Bartlett
Wm. Whipple
Matthew Thornton

Massachusetts Bay

Saml. Adams
John Adams
Robt. Treat Paine
Elbridge Gerry

Rhode Island

Step. Hopkins
William Ellery

Connecticut

Roger Sherman
Saml. Huntington
Wm. Williams
Oliver Wolcott

New York

Wm. Floyd
Phil. Livingston
Frans. Lewis
Lewis Morris

New Jersey

Richd. Stockton
Jno. Witherspoon
Fras. Hopkinson
John Hart
Abra. Clark

Pennsylvania

Robt. Morris
Benjamin Rush
Benja. Franklin
John Morton
Geo. Clymer
Jas. Smith
Geo. Taylor
James Wilson
Geo. Ross

Delaware

Caesar Rodney
Geo. Read
Tho. M'Kean

Maryland

Samuel Chase
Wm. Paca
Thos. Stone
Charles Carroll
of Carrollton

Virginia

George Wythe
Richard Henry Lee
Th. Jefferson
Benja. Harrison
Thos. Nelson Jr.
Francis Lightfoot Lee
Carter Braxton

North Carolina

Wm. Hooper
Joseph Hewes
John Penn

South Carolina

Edward Rutledge
Thos. Heyward Junr.
Thomas Lynch Junr.
Arthur Middleton

Georgia

Button Gwinnett
Lyman Hall
Geo. Walton

Constitution of the United States of America*

PREAMBLE

We the People of the United States, in order to form a more perfect Union, establish justice, insure domestic tranquility, provide for the common defense, promote the general welfare, and secure the blessings of liberty to ourselves and our posterity, do ordain and establish this Constitution for the United States of America.

ARTICLE I

Section 1. All legislative powers herein granted shall be vested in a Congress of the United States, which shall consist of a Senate and House of Representatives.

Section 2. The House of Representatives shall be composed of members chosen every second year by the people of the several States, and the electors in each State shall have the qualifications requisite for electors of the most numerous branch of the State Legislature.

No person shall be a representative who shall not have attained to the age of twenty-five years, and been seven years a citizen of the United States, and who shall not, when elected, be an inhabitant of that State in which he shall be chosen.

Representatives and direct taxes shall be apportioned among the several States which may be included within this Union, according to their respective numbers, which shall be determined by adding to the whole number of free persons, including those bound to service for a term of years, and excluding Indians not taxed, three-fifths of all other persons. The actual enumeration shall be made within three years after the first meeting of the Congress of the United States, and within every subsequent term of ten years, in such manner as they shall by law direct. The number of representatives shall not exceed one for every thirty thousand, but each State shall have at least one representative; and until such enumeration shall be made, the State of New Hampshire shall be entitled to choose three, Massachusetts eight, Rhode Island and Providence Plantations one, Connecticut five, New York six, New Jersey four, Pennsylvania eight, Delaware one, Maryland six, Virginia ten, North Carolina five, South Carolina five, and Georgia three.

When vacancies happen in the representation from any State, the Executive authority thereof shall issue writs of election to fill such vacancies.

The House of Representatives shall choose their Speaker and other officers; and shall have the sole power of impeachment.

SECTION 3. The Senate of the United States shall be composed of two senators from each State, chosen by the legislature thereof, for six years and each senator shall have one vote.

Immediately after they shall be assembled in consequence of the first election, they shall be divided as equally as may be into three classes. The seats of the senators of the first class shall be vacated at the expiration of the second year, of the second class at the expiration of the fourth year, and of the third class at the expiration of the sixth year, so that one-third may be chosen every second year; and if vacancies happen by resignation, or otherwise, during the recess of the legislature of any State, the executive thereof may make temporary appointments until the next meeting of the legislature, which shall then fill such vacancies.

No person shall be a senator who shall not have attained to the age of thirty years, and been nine years a citizen of the United States, and who shall not, when elected, be an inhabitant of that State for which he shall be chosen.

The Vice President of the United States shall be President of the Senate, but shall have no vote, unless they be equally divided.

The Senate shall choose their other officers, and also a President pro tempore, in the absence of the Vice President, or when he shall exercise the office of President of the United States.

The Senate shall have the sole power to try all impeachments. When sitting for that purpose, they shall be on oath or affirmation. When the President of the United States is tried, the Chief Justice shall preside: And no person shall be convicted without the concurrence of two thirds of the members present.

Judgment in cases of impeachment shall not extend further than to removal from office, and disqualification to hold and enjoy any office or honor, trust or profit under the United States: but the party convicted shall nevertheless be liable and subject to indictment, trial, judgment and punishment, according to law.

SECTION 4. The times, places and manner of holding elections for senators and representatives, shall be prescribed in each State by the legislature thereof; but the Congress may at any time by law make or alter such regulations, except as to the places of choosing senators.

The Congress shall assemble at least once in every year, and such meeting shall be on the first Monday in December, unless they shall by law appoint a different day.

SECTION 5. Each house shall be the judge of the elections, returns and qualifications of its own members, and a majority of each shall constitute a quorum to do business; but a smaller number may adjourn from day to day, and may be authorized to compel the attendance of absent members, in such manner, and under such penalties as each house may provide.

Each house may determine the rules of its proceedings, punish its members for disorderly behaviour, and, with the concurrence of two-thirds, expel a member.

Each house shall keep a journal of its proceedings, and from time to time publish the same, excepting such parts as may in their judgment require secrecy; and the yeas and the nays of the members of either house on any question shall, at the desire of one-fifth of those present, be entered on the journal.

Neither house, during the session of Congress, shall, without the consent of the other, adjourn for more than three days, nor to any other place than that in which the two houses shall be sitting.

SECTION 6. The senators and representatives shall receive a

compensation for their services, to be ascertained by law, and paid out of the Treasury of the United States. They shall in all cases, except treason, felony and breach of the peace, be privileged from arrest during their attendance at the session of their respective houses, and in going to and returning from the same; and for any speech or debate in either house, they shall not be questioned in any other place.

No senator or representative shall, during the time for which he was elected, be appointed to any civil office under the authority of the United States, which shall have been created, or the emoluments whereof shall have been increased during such time; and no person holding any office under the United States, shall be a member of either house during his continuance in office.

Section 7. All bills for raising revenue shall originate in the House of Representatives; but the Senate may propose or concur with amendments as on other bills.

Every bill which shall have passed the House of Representatives and the Senate, shall, before it become a law, be presented to the President of the United States; if he approves he shall sign it, but if not he shall return it, with his objections to that house in which it shall have originated, who shall enter for the objections at large on their journal, and proceed to reconsider it. If after such reconsideration two thirds of that House shall agree to pass the bill, it shall be sent, together with the objections, to the other House, by which it shall likewise be reconsidered, and if approved by two thirds of that House, it shall become a law. But in all cases the votes of both Houses shall be determined by yeas and nays, and the names of the persons voting for and against the bill shall be entered on the journal of each House respectively. If any bill shall not be returned by the President within ten days (Sundays excepted) after it shall have been presented to him, the same shall be a law, in like manner as if he had signed it, unless the Congress by their adjournment prevent its return, in which case it shall not be a law.

Every order, resolution, or vote to which the concurrence of the Senate and House of Representatives may be necessary (except on a question of adjournment) shall be presented to the

President of the United States; and before the same shall take effect, shall be approved by him, or being disapproved by him, shall be repassed by two thirds of the Senate and House of Representatives, according to the rules and limitations prescribed in the case of a bill.

SECTION 8. The Congress shall have power to lay and collect taxes, duties, imposts and excises, to pay the debts and provide for the common defense and general welfare of the United States; but all duties, imposts and excises shall be uniform throughout the United States;

To borrow money on the credit of the United States;

To regulate commerce with foreign nations, and among the several States, and with the Indian tribes;

To establish a uniform rule of naturalization, and uniform laws on the subject of bankruptcies throughout the United States;

To coin money, regulate the value thereof, and of foreign coin, and fix the standard of weights and measures;

To provide for the punishment of counterfeiting the securities and current coin of the United States;

To establish post offices and post roads;

To promote the progress of science and useful arts, by securing for limited times to authors and inventors the exclusive right to their respective writings and discoveries;

To constitute tribunals inferior to the Supreme Court;

To define and punish piracies and felonies committed on the high seas, and offenses against the law of nations;

To declare war, grant letters of marque and reprisal, and make rules concerning captures on land and water;

To raise and support armies, but no appropriation of money to that use shall be for a longer term than two years;

To provide and maintain a Navy;

To make rules for the government and regulation of the land and naval forces;

To provide for calling forth the militia to execute the laws of the Union, suppress insurrections and repel invasions;

To provide for organizing, arming, and disciplining the militia, and for governing such part of them as may be employed in the service of the United States, reserving to the States respectively, the appointment of the officers, and the authority of training the militia according to the discipline prescribed by Congress;

To exercise exclusive legislation in all cases whatsoever, over such district (not exceeding ten miles square) as may, by cession of particular States, and the acceptance of Congress, become the seat of the Government of the United States, and to exercise like authority over all places purchased by the consent of the legislature of the State in which the same shall be, for the erection of forts, magazines, arsenals, dock-yards, and other needful buildings;—And

To make all laws which shall be necessary and proper for carrying into execution the foregoing powers and all other powers vested by this Constitution in the Government of the United States, or in any department or officer thereof.

Section 9. The migration of importation of such persons as any of the States now existing shall think proper to admit, shall not be prohibited by the Congress prior to the year one thousand eight hundred and eight, but a tax or duty may be imposed on such importation, not exceeding ten dollars for each person.

The privilege of the writ of habeas corpus shall not be suspended, unless when in cases of rebellion or invasion the public safety may require it.

No bill of attainder or ex post facto law shall be passed.

No capitation, or other direct, tax shall be laid, unless in proportion to the census or enumeration herein before directed to be taken.

No tax or duty shall be laid on articles exported from any State.

No preference shall be given by any regulation of commerce or revenue to the ports of one State over those of another: nor shall vessels bound to, or from, one State, be obliged to enter, clear, or pay duties in another.

No money shall be drawn from the Treasury, but in consequence of appropriations made by law; and a regular statement and account of the receipts and expenditures of all public money shall be published from time to time.

No title of nobility shall be granted by the United States: And no person holding any office of profit or trust under them, shall, without the consent of the Congress, accept of any present, emolument, office, or title, of any kind whatever, from any King, Prince, or foreign State.

SECTION 10. No State shall enter into any treaty, alliance, or confederation, grant letters of marque and reprisal; coin money; emit bills of credit; make any thing but gold and silver coin a tender in payment of debts; pass any bill of attainder, ex post facto law, or law impairing the obligation of contracts, or grant any title of nobility.

No State shall, without the consent of the Congress, lay any imposts or duties on imports or exports, except what may be absolutely necessary for executing its inspection laws: and the net produce of all duties and imposts, laid by any State on imports or exports, shall be for the use of the Treasury of the United States; and all such laws shall be subject to the revision and control of the Congress.

No State shall, without the consent of Congress, lay any duty of tonnage, keep troops, or ships of war in time of peace, enter into any agreement or compact with another State, or with a foreign power, or engage in war, unless actually invaded, or in such imminent danger as will not admit of delay.

ARTICLE II

SECTION 1. The executive power shall be vested in a President of the United States of America. He shall hold his office during the term of four years, and, together with the Vice President, chosen for the same term, be elected, as follows:

Each State, shall appoint, in such manner as the legislature thereof may direct, a number of electors, equal to the whole number of senators and representatives to which the State may be entitled in the Congress; but no senator or representative, or person holding an office of trust or profit under the United States, shall be appointed an elector.

The electors shall meet in their respective States, and vote by ballot for two persons, of whom one at least shall not be an inhabitant of the same State with themselves. And they shall make a list of all the persons voted for, and of the number of votes for each; which list they shall sign and certify, and transmit sealed to the seat of the Government of the United States, directed to the President of the Senate. The President of the Senate shall, in the presence of the Senate and House of Representatives, open all the certificates, and the votes shall then be counted. The person having the greatest number of votes shall be the President, if such number be a majority of the whole number of electors appointed; and if there be more than one who have such majority, and have an equal number of votes, then the House of Representatives shall immediately choose by ballot one of them for President; and if no person have a majority, then from the five highest on the list the said House shall in like manner choose the President. But in choosing the President, the votes shall be taken by States, the representation from each State having one vote; a quorum for this purpose shall consist of a member or members from two thirds of the States, and a majority of all the States shall be necessary to a choice. In every case, after the choice of the President, the person having the greatest number of votes of the electors shall be the Vice President. But if there should remain two or more who have equal votes, the Senate shall choose from them by ballot the Vice President.

The Congress may determine the time of choosing the electors, and the day on which they shall give their votes; which day shall be the same throughout the United States.

No person except a natural born citizen, or a citizen of the United States, at the time of the adoption of this Constitution, shall be eligible to the office of President; neither shall any person be eligible to that office who shall not have attained to the age of thirty-five years, and been fourteen years a resident within the United States.

In case of the removal of the President from office, or of his death, resignation, or inability to discharge the powers and duties of the said office, the same shall devolve on the Vice

President, and the Congress may by law provide for the case of removal, death, resignation, or inability, both of the President and Vice President, declaring what officer shall then act as President, and such officer shall act accordingly, until the disability be removed, or a President shall be elected.

The President shall, at stated times, receive for his services, a compensation, which shall neither be increased nor diminished during the period for which he shall have been elected, and he shall not receive within that period any other emolument from the United States, or any of them.

Before he enter on the execution of his office, he shall take the following oath or affirmation:—"I do solemnly swear (or affirm) that I will faithfully execute the office of President of the United States, and will to the best of my ability, preserve, protect and defend the Constitution of the United States."

SECTION 2. The President shall be Commander in Chief of the Army and Navy of the United States, and of the militia of the several States, when called into the actual service of the United States; he may require the opinion, in writing, of the principal officer in each of the Executive Departments, upon any subject relating to the duties of their respective offices, and he shall have power to grant reprieves and pardons for offenses against the United States, except in cases of impeachment.

He shall have power, by and with the advice and consent of the Senate, to make treaties, provided two-thirds of the Senators present concur; and he shall nominate, and by and with the advice and consent of the Senate, shall appoint ambassadors, other public ministers and consuls, Judges of the Supreme Court, and all other officers of the United States, whose appointments are not herein otherwise provided for, and which shall be established by law: but the Congress may by law vest the appointment of such inferior officers, as they think proper, in the President alone, in the courts of law, or in the heads of departments.

The President shall have power to fill up all vacancies that may happen during the recess of the Senate, by granting commissions which shall expire at the end of their next session.

SECTION 3. He shall from time to time give to the Congress information of the state of the Union, and recommend to their consideration such measures as he shall judge necessary and expedient; he may, on extraordinary occasions, convene both houses, or either of them, and in case of disagreement between them, with respect to the time of adjournment, he may adjourn them to such time as he shall think proper; he shall receive ambassadors and other public ministers; he shall take care that the laws be faithfully executed, and shall commission all the officers of the United States.

SECTION 4. The President, Vice President and all civil officers of the United States, shall be removed from office on impeachment for, and conviction of, treason, bribery, or other high crimes and misdemeanors.

ARTICLE III

SECTION 1. The judicial power of the United States, shall be vested in one Supreme Court, and in such inferior courts as the Congress may from time to time ordain and establish. The judges, both of the supreme and inferior courts, shall hold their offices during good behaviour, and shall, at stated times, receive for their services, a compensation, which shall not be diminished during their continuance in office.

SECTION 2. The judicial power shall extend to all cases, in law and equity, arising under this Constitution, the laws of the United States, and treaties made, or which shall be made, under their authority;—to all cases affecting ambassadors, other public ministers and consuls;—to all cases of admiralty and maritime jurisdiction;—to controversies to which the United States shall be a party;—to controversies between two or more States;—between a State and citizens of another State;—between citizens of different States,—between citizens of the same State claiming lands under grants of different States, and between a State, or the citizens thereof, and foreign States, citizens or subjects.

In all cases affecting ambassadors, other public ministers and consuls, and those in which a State shall be a party, the Supreme Court shall have original jurisdiction. In all the other cases before mentioned, the Supreme Court shall have appellate jurisdiction, both as to law and fact, with such exceptions, and under such regulations as the Congress shall make.

The trial of all crimes, except in cases of impeachment, shall be by jury; and such trial shall be held in the State where the said crimes shall have been committed; but when not committed within any State, the trial shall be at such place or places as the Congress may by law have directed.

SECTION 3. Treason against the United States, shall consist only in levying war against them, or in adhering to their enemies, giving them aid and comfort. No person shall be convicted of treason unless on the testimony of two witnesses to the same overt act, or on confession in open court.

The Congress shall have power to declare the punishment of treason, but no attainder of treason shall work corruption of blood, or forfeiture except during the life of the person attained.

ARTICLE IV

SECTION 1. Full faith and credit shall be given in each State to the public acts, records, and judicial proceedings of every other State. And the Congress may by general laws prescribe the manner in which such acts, records and proceedings shall be proved, and the effect thereof.

SECTION 2. The citizens of each State shall be entitled to all privileges and immunities of citizens in the several States.

A person charged in any State with treason, felony, or other crime, who shall flee from justice, and be found in another State, shall on demand of the executive authority of the State from which he fled, be delivered up, to be removed to the State having jurisdiction of the crime.

No person held to service or labour in one State, under the laws thereof; escaping into another, shall, in consequence of any law or regulation therein, be discharged from such service or labour, but shall be delivered up on claim of the party to whom such service or labour may be due.

SECTION 3. New States may be admitted by the Congress into this Union; but no new State shall be formed or erected within the jurisdiction of any other State; nor any State be formed by the junction of two or more States, or parts of States, without the consent of the legislatures of the States concerned as well as of the Congress.

The Congress shall have power to dispose of and make all needful rules and regulations respecting the Territory or other property belonging to the United States; and nothing in this Constitution shall be so construed as to prejudice any claims of the United States, or of any particular State.

SECTION 4. The United States shall guarantee to every State in this Union a republican form of Government, and shall protect each of them against invasion; and on application of the legislature, or of the executive (when the legislature cannot be convened) against domestic violence.

ARTICLE V

The Congress, whenever two third of both Houses shall deem it necessary, shall propose amendments to this Constitution, or on the application of the legislatures of two thirds of the several States, shall call a convention for proposing amendments, which, in either case, shall be valid to all intents and purposes, as part of this Constitution, when ratified by the legislatures of three fourths of the several States, or by conventions in three fourths thereof, as the one or the other mode of ratification may be proposed by the Congress; provided that no amendment which may be made prior to the year one thousand eight hundred and eight shall in any manner affect the first and fourth clauses in the Ninth Section of the First Article; and that no State, without its consent, shall be deprived of its equal suffrage in the Senate.

ARTICLE VI

All debts contracted and engagements entered into, before the adoption of this Constitution, shall be as valid against the United States under this Constitution, as under the Confederation.

This Constitution, and the laws of the United States which shall be made in pursuance thereof; and all treaties made, or which shall be made, under the authority of the United States, shall be the supreme law of the land; and the judges in every State shall be bound thereby, any thing in the Constitution or laws of any State to the contrary notwithstanding.

The senators and representatives before mentioned, and the members of the several State legislatures, and all executive and judicial officers, both of the United States and of the several States, shall be bound by oath or affirmation, to support this Constitution; but no religious test shall ever be required as a qualification to any office or public trust under the United States.

ARTICLE VII

The ratification of the conventions of nine States shall be sufficient for the establishment of this Constitution between the States so ratifying the same.

Done in convention by the unanimous consent of the States present the seventeenth day of September in the year of our Lord one thousand seven hundred and eighty seven and of the Independence of the United States of America the twelfth. In witness whereof we have hereunto subscribed our names,

Go. Washington—*Presid't.*
and deputy from Virginia

Attest William Jackson—*Secretary*

New Hampshire

John Langdon | Nicholas Gilman

Massachusetts

Nathaniel Gorham | Rufus King

Connecticut

Wm. Saml. Johnson | Roger Sherman

New York

Alexander Hamilton

New Jersey

Wil. Livingston | Wm. Paterson
David Brearley | Jona. Dayton

Pennsylvania

B. Franklin | Thos. FitzSimons
Thomas Mifflin | Jared Ingersoll
Robt. Morris | James Wilson
Geo. Clymer | Gouv. Morris

Delaware

Geo. Read | Richard Bassett
Gunning Bedford Jun | Jaco. Broom
John Dickinson

Maryland

James McHenry | Danl. Carroll
Dan. of St. Thos. Jenifer

Virginia

John Blair | James Madison Jr.

North Carolina

Wm. Blount | Hu. Williamson
Richd. Dobbs Spaight

South Carolina

J. Rutledge | Charles Pinckney
Charles Cotesworth Pinckney | Pierce Butler

Georgia

William Few | Abr. Baldwin

Amendments

ARTICLE I

Congress shall make no law respecting an establishment of religion, or prohibiting the free exercise thereof; or abridging the freedom of speech, or of the press; or the right of the people peaceably to assemble, and to petition the Government for a redress of grievances.

ARTICLE II

A well regulated militia, being necessary to the security of a free State, the right of the people to keep and bear arms, shall not be infringed.

ARTICLE III

No soldier shall, in time of peace be quartered in any house, without the consent of the owner, nor in time of war, but in a manner to be prescribed by law.

ARTICLE IV

The right of the people to be secure in their persons, houses, papers, and effects, against unreasonable searches and seizures, shall not be violated, and no warrants shall issue, but upon probable cause, supported by oath or affirmation, and particularly describing the place to be searched, and the persons or things to be seized.

ARTICLE V

No person shall be held to answer for a capital, or otherwise infamous crime, unless on a presentment or indictment of a Grand Jury, except in cases arising in the land or naval forces, or in the militia, when in actual service in time of war or public danger; nor shall any person be subject for the same offense to be twice put in jeopardy of life or limb; nor shall be compelled in any criminal case to be a witness against himself, nor be deprived of life, liberty, or property, without due process of law; nor shall private property be taken for public use, without just compensation.

ARTICLE VI

In all criminal prosecutions, the accused shall enjoy the right to a speedy and public trial, by an impartial jury of the State and district wherein the crime shall have been committed, which district shall have been previously ascertained by law, and to be informed of the nature and cause of the accusation; to be confronted with the witnesses against him; to have compulsory process for obtaining witnesses in his favor, and to have the assistance of counsel for his defense.

ARTICLE VII

In suits at common law, where the value in controversy shall exceed twenty dollars, the right of trial by jury shall be preserved, and no fact tried by a jury, shall be otherwise reexamined in any court of the United States, than according to the rules of the common law.

ARTICLE VIII

Excessive bail shall not be required, nor excessive fines imposed, nor cruel and unusual punishments inflicted.

ARTICLE IX

The enumeration in the Constitution, of certain rights, shall not be construed to deny or disparage others retained by the people.

ARTICLE X

The powers not delegated to the United States by the Constitution, nor prohibited by it to the States, are reserved to the States respectively, or to the people.

ARTICLE XI

The judicial power of the United States shall not be construed to extend to any suit in law or equity, commenced or prosecuted against one of the United States by citizens of another State, or by citizens or subjects of any foreign State.

ARTICLE XII

The electors shall meet in their respective States, and vote by ballot for President and Vice President, one of whom, at least, shall not be an inhabitant of the same State with themselves; they shall name in their ballots the person voted for as President, and in distinct ballots the person voted for as Vice President, and they shall make distinct lists of all persons voted for as President, and of all persons voted for as Vice President, and of the number of votes for each, which lists they shall sign and certify, and transmit sealed to the seat of the government of the United States, directed to the President of the Senate;—The President of the Senate shall, in the presence of the Senate and House of Representatives, open all the certificates and the votes shall then be counted;—The person having the greatest number of votes for President, shall be the President, if such number be a majority of the whole number of electors appointed; and if no person have such majority, then from the persons having the highest numbers not exceeding three on the list of those voted for as President, the House of Representatives shall choose immediately, by ballot, the President. But in choosing the President, the votes shall be taken by States, the representation from each State having one vote; a quorum for this purpose shall consist of a member or members from two-thirds of the States, and a majority of all the States shall be necessary to a choice. And if the House of Representatives shall not choose a President whenever the right of choice shall devolve upon them, before the fourth day of March next following, then the Vice President shall act as President, as in the case of the death or other constitutional disability of the President.—The person having the greatest number of votes as Vice President, shall be the Vice President, if such number be a majority of the whole number of electors appointed, and if no person have a majority, then from the two highest numbers on the list, the Senate shall choose the Vice President; a quorum for the purpose shall consist of two-thirds of the whole number of Senators, and a majority of the whole number shall be necessary to a choice. But no person constitutionally ineligible to the office of President shall be eligible to that of Vice President of the United States.

ARTICLE XIII

SECTION 1. Neither slavery nor involuntary servitude, except as a punishment for crime whereof the party shall have been duly convicted, shall exist within the United States, or any place subject to their jurisdiction.

SECTION 2. Congress shall have power to enforce this article by appropriate legislation.

ARTICLE XIV

SECTION 1. All persons born or naturalized in the United States, and subject to the jurisdiction thereof, are citizens of the United States and of the State wherein they reside. No State shall make or enforce any law which shall abridge the privileges or immunities of citizens of the United States; nor shall any State deprive any person of life, liberty, or property, without due process of law; nor deny to any person within its jurisdiction the equal protection of the laws.

SECTION 2. Representatives shall be apportioned among the several States according to their respective numbers, counting the whole number of persons in each State, excluding Indians not taxed. But when the right to vote at any election for the choice of electors for President and Vice President of the United States, Representatives in Congress, the executive and judicial officers of a State, or the members of the legislature thereof, is denied to any of the male inhabitants of such State, being twenty-one years of age, and citizens of the United States, or in any way abridged, except for participation in rebellion, or other crime, the basis of representation therein shall be reduced in the proportion which the number of such male citizens shall bear to the whole number of male citizens twenty-one years of age in such State.

SECTION 3. No person shall be a Senator or Representative in Congress, or elector of President and Vice President, or hold any office, civil or military, under the United States, or under any State, who, having previously taken an oath, as a member of Congress, or as an officer of the United States, or as a member of any State legislature, or as an executive or judicial officer of any State, to support the Constitution of the United States, shall have engaged in insurrection or rebellion against the same, or given aid or comfort to the enemies thereof. But Congress may by a vote of two-thirds of each house, remove such disability.

SECTION 4. The validity of the public debt of the United States, authorized by law, including debts incurred for payment of pensions and bounties for services in suppressing insurrection or rebellion, shall not be questioned. But neither the United States nor any State shall assume or pay any debt or obligation incurred in aid of insurrection or rebellion against the United States, or any claim for the loss or emancipation of any slave; but all such debts, obligations and claims shall be held illegal and void.

SECTION 5. The Congress shall have power to enforce, by appropriate legislation, the provisions of this article.

ARTICLE XV

SECTION 1. The right of citizens of the United States to vote shall not be denied or abridged by the United States or by any State on account of race, color, or previous condition of servitude.

SECTION 2. The Congress shall have power to enforce this article by appropriate legislation.

ARTICLE XVI

The Congress shall have power to lay and collect taxes on incomes, from whatever source derived, without apportionment among the several States, and without regard to any census or enumeration.

ARTICLE XVII

SECTION 1. The Senate of the United States shall be composed of two senators from each State, elected by the people thereof, for six years; and each senator shall have one vote. The electors in each State shall have the qualifications requisite for electors of the most numerous branch of the State legislatures.

SECTION 2. When vacancies happen in the representation of any State in the senate, the executive authority of such State shall issue writs of election to fill such vacancies: *Provided,* That the legislature of any State may empower the executive thereof to make temporary appointments until the people fill the vacancies by election as the legislature may direct.

SECTION 3. This amendment shall not be so construed as to affect the election or term of any senator chosen before it becomes valid as part of the Constitution.

ARTICLE XVIII

SECTION 1. After one year from the ratification of this article the manufacture, sale, or transportation of intoxicating liquors within, the importation thereof into, or the exportation thereof from the United States and all territory subject to the jurisdiction thereof for beverage purposes is hereby prohibited.

SECTION 2. The Congress and the several States shall have concurrent power to enforce this article by appropriate legislation.

SECTION 3. This article shall be inoperative unless it shall have been ratified as an amendment to the Constitution by the legislatures of the several States, as provided in the Constitution, within seven years from the date of the submission hereof to the States by the Congress.

ARTICLE XIX

SECTION 1. The right of citizens of the United States to vote shall not be denied or abridged by the United States or by any State on account of sex.

ARTICLE XX

SECTION 1. The terms of the President and Vice President shall end at noon on the 20th day of January, and the terms of Senators and Representatives at noon on the 3d day of January, of the years in which such terms would have ended if this article had not been ratified; and the terms of their successors shall then begin.

SECTION 2. The Congress shall assemble at least once in every year, and such meeting shall begin at noon on the 3d day of January, unless they shall by law appoint a different day.

SECTION 3. If, at the time fixed for the beginning of the term of the President, the President elect shall have died, the Vice President elect shall become President. If a President shall not have been chosen before the time fixed for the beginning of his term, or if the President elect shall have failed to qualify, then the Vice President elect shall act as President until a President shall have qualified; and the Congress may by law provide for the case wherein neither a President elect nor a Vice President elect shall have qualified, declaring who shall then act as President, or the manner in which one who is to act shall be selected, and such person shall act accordingly until a President or Vice President shall have qualified.

SECTION 4. The Congress may by law provide for the case of the death of any of the persons from whom the House of Representatives may choose a President whenever the right of choice shall have devolved upon them, and for the case of the death of any of the persons from whom the Senate may choose a Vice President whenever the right of choice shall have devolved upon them.

SECTION 5. Sections 1 and 2 shall take effect on the 15th day of October following the ratification of this article.

SECTION 6. This article shall be inoperative unless it shall have been ratified as an amendment to the Constitution by the legislatures of three-fourths of the several States within seven years from the date of its submission.

ARTICLE XXI

SECTION 1. The eighteenth article of amendment to the Constitution of the United States is hereby repealed.

SECTION 2. The transportation or importation into any State, Territory, or possession of the United States for delivery or use therein of intoxicating liquors, in violation of the laws thereof, is hereby prohibited.

SECTION 3. This article shall be inoperative unless it shall have been ratified as an amendment to the Constitution by conventions in the several States, as provided in the Constitution, within seven years from the date of the submission hereof to the States by the Congress.

ARTICLE XXII

SECTION 1. No person shall be elected to the office of the President more than twice, and no person who has held the office of President, or acted as President, for more than 2 years of a term to which some other person was elected President shall be elected to the office of the President more than once. But this Article shall not apply to any person holding the office of President when this Article was proposed by the Congress, and shall not prevent any person who may be holding the office of President, or acting as President, during the term within which this Article becomes operative from holding the office of President or acting as President during the remainder of such term.

SECTION 2. This Article shall be inoperative unless it shall have been ratified as an amendment to the Constitution by the legislatures of three-fourths of the several States within 7 years from the date of its submission to the States by the Congress.

ARTICLE XXIII

SECTION 1. The District constituting the seat of Government of the United States shall appoint in such manner as the Congress may direct:

A number of electors of President and Vice President equal to the whole number of Senators and Representatives in Congress to which the District would be entitled if it were a State, but in no event more than the least populous State; they shall be in addition to those appointed by the States, but they shall be considered, for the purposes of the election of President and Vice President, to be electors appointed by a State; and they shall meet in the District and perform such duties as provided by the twelfth article of amendment.

SECTION 2. The Congress shall have power to enforce this article by appropriate legislation.

ARTICLE XXIV

SECTION 1. The right of citizens of the United States to vote in any primary or other election for President or Vice President, for electors for President or Vice President, or for Senator or Representative in Congress, shall not be denied or abridged by the United States or any State by reason of failure to pay any poll tax or other tax.

SECTION 2. The Congress shall have power to enforce this article by appropriate legislation.

ARTICLE XXV

SECTION 1. In case of the removal of the President from office or of his death or resignation, the Vice President shall become President.

SECTION 2. Whenever there is a vacancy in the office of the Vice President, the President shall nominate a Vice President who shall take office upon confirmation by a majority vote of both Houses of Congress.

SECTION 3. Whenever the President transmits to the President pro tempore of the Senate and the Speaker of the House of Representatives his written declaration that he is unable to discharge the powers and duties of his office, and until he transmits to them a written declaration to the contrary, such powers and duties shall be discharged by the Vice President as Acting President.

SECTION 4. Whenever the Vice President and a majority of either the principal officers of the executive departments or of such other body as Congress may by law provide, transmit to the President pro tempore of the Senate and the Speaker of the House of Representatives their written declaration that the President is unable to discharge the powers and duties of his office, the Vice President shall immediately assume the powers and duties of the office as Acting President.

Thereafter, when the President transmits to the President pro tempore of the Senate and the Speaker of the House of Representatives his written declaration that no inability exists, he shall resume the powers and duties of his office unless the Vice President and a majority of either the principal officers of the executive department or of such other body as Congress may by law provide, transmit within four days to the President pro tempore of the Senate and the Speaker of the House of Representatives their written declaration that the President is unable to discharge the powers and duties of his office. Thereupon Congress shall decide the issue, assembling within forty-eight hours for that purpose if not in session. If the Congress, within twenty-one days after receipt of the latter written declaration, or if Congress is not in session, within twenty-one days after Congress is required to assemble, determines by two-thirds vote of both Houses that the President is unable to discharge the powers and duties of his office, the Vice President shall continue to discharge the same as Acting President; otherwise, the President shall resume the powers and duties of his office.

ARTICLE XXVI

SECTION 1. The right of citizens of the United States, who are eighteen years of age or older, to vote shall not be denied or abridged by the United States or by any state on account of age.

SECTION 2. The Congress shall have power to enforce this article by appropriate legislation.

Constitución de los Estados Unidos de América

PREAMBULO

Nosotros, el Pueblo de los Estados Unidos, a fin de formar una Unión más perfecta, establecer la justicia, garantizar la tranquilidad nacional, atender a la defensa común, fomentar el bienestar general y asegurar los beneficios de la libertad para nosotros y para nuestra posteridad, por la presente promulgamos y establecemos esta Constitución para los Estados Unidos de América.

ARTICULO I

SECCION 1. Todos los poderes legislativos otorgados por esta Constitución residirán en un Congreso de los Estados Unidos que se compondrá de un Senado y de una Cámara de Representantes.

SECCION 2. La Cámara de Representantes se compondrá de miembros elegidos cada dos años por el pueblo de los distintos estados, y los electores en cada estado cumplirán con los requisitos exigidos a los electores de la Cámara más numerosa de la Asamblea Legislativa de dicho estado.

No podrá ser representante ninguna persona que no haya cumplido veinticinco años de edad, que no haya sido durante siete años ciudadano de los Estados Unidos y que al tiempo de su elección no resida en el estado que ha de elegirlo.

Tanto los representantes como las contribuciones directas se prorratearán entre los diversos estados que integren esta Unión, en relación al número respectivo de sus habitantes, el cual se determinará añadiendo al número total de personas libres, en el que se incluye a las que estén obligadas al servicio por determinado número de años y se excluye a los indios que no paguen contribuciones, las tres quintas partes de todas las demás. Se efectuará el censo dentro de los tres años siguientes a la primera reunión del Congreso de los Estados Unidos, y en lo sucesivo cada diez años, en la forma en que éste lo dispusiere por ley. No habrá más de un representante por cada treinta mil habitantes, pero cada estado tendrá por lo menos un representante. En tanto se realiza el censo, el Estado de Nueva Hampshire tendrá derecho a elegir tres representantes; Massachusetts, ocho; Rhode Island y las Plantaciones de Providence, uno; Connecticut, cinco; Nueva York, seis; Nueva Jersey, cuatro; Pensilvania, ocho; Delaware, uno; Maryland, seis; Virginia, diez; Carolina del Norte, cinco; Carolina del Sur, cinco y Georgia, tres.

Cuando ocurrieren vacantes en la representación de cualquier estado, la autoridad ejecutiva de éste ordenará la celebración de elecciones para cubrirlas.

La Cámara de Representantes elegirá su Presidente y demás funcionarios y sólo ella tendrá la facultad de iniciar procedimientos de residencia.

SECCION 3. El Senado de los Estados Unidos se compondrá de dos senadores por cada estado, elegidos por sus respectivas Asambleas Legislativas por el término de seis años. Cada senador tendrá derecho a un voto.

Tan pronto como se reúnan en virtud de la primera elección, se les dividirá en tres grupos lo más iguales posible. El término de los senadores del primer grupo expirará al finalizar el segundo año; el del segundo grupo al finalizar el cuarto año y el del tercer grupo al finalizar el sexto año, de forma que cada dos años se renueve una tercera parte de sus miembros. Si ocurrieren vacantes, por renuncia o por cualquier otra causa, mientras esté en receso la Asamblea Legislativa del estado respectivo, la autoridad ejecutiva del mismo podrá hacer nombramientos provisionales hasta la próxima sesión de la Asamblea Legislativa, la que entonces cubrirá tales vacantes.

No podrá ser senador quien no haya cumplido treinta años de edad, no haya sido durante nueve años ciudadano de los Estados Unidos y no resida, en la época de su elección, en el estado que ha de elegirlo.

El vicepresidente de los Estados Unidos será Presidente del Senado, pero no tendrá voto, excepto en caso de empate.

El Senado elegirá sus demás funcionarios así como también un presidente pro témpore en ausencia del vicepresidente o cuando éste desempeñare el cargo de Presidente de los Estados Unidos.

Tan sólo el Senado podrá conocer de procedimientos de residencia. Cuando se reúna para este fin, los senadores prestarán juramento o harán promesa de cumplir fielmente su cometido. Si se residenciare al Presidente de los Estados Unidos, presidirá la sesión el Juez Presidente del Tribunal Supremo. Nadie será convicto sin que concurran las dos terceras partes de los senadores presentes.

La sentencia en procedimientos de residencia no podrá exceder de la destitución del cargo e inhabilitación para obtener y desempeñar ningún cargo de honor, de confianza o de retribución en el Gobierno de los Estados Unidos; pero el funcionario convicto quedará, no obstante, sujeto a ser acusado, juzgado, sentenciado y castigado con arreglo a derecho.

SECCION 4. La Asamblea Legislativa de cada estado determinará la fecha, lugar y modo de celebrar las elecciones de senadores y representantes; pero el Congreso podrá en cualquier momento mediante legislación adecuada aprobar o modificar tales disposiciones, salvo en relación al lugar donde se habrá de elegir a los senadores.

El Congreso se reunirá por lo menos una vez al año y tal sesión comenzará el primer lunes de diciembre, a no ser que por ley se fije otro día.

SECCION 5. Cada Cámara será el único juez de las elecciones, resultado de las mismas y capacidad de sus propios miembros; y la mayoría de cada una de ellas constituirá quorum para realizar sus trabajos; pero un número menor podrá recesar de día en día y estará autorizado para compeler la asistencia de los miembros ausentes, en la forma y bajo las penalidades que cada Cámara determinare.

Cada Cámara adoptará su reglamento, podrá castigar a sus miembros por conducta impropia y expulsarlos con el voto de dos terceras partes. Cada Cámara tendrá un diario de sesiones, que publicará periódicamente, con excepción de aquello que, a su juicio, deba mantenerse en secreto; y siempre que así lo pidiere la quinta parte de los miembros presentes, se harán constar en dicho diario los votos afirmativos y negativos de los miembros de una u otra Cámara sobre cualquier asunto.

Mientras el Congreso estuviere reunido, ninguna Cámara podrá, sin el consentimiento de la otra, levantar sus sesiones por más de tres días ni reunirse en otro lugar que no sea aquél en que las dos estén instaladas.

SECCION 6. Los senadores y representantes recibirán por sus servicios una remuneración fijada por ley y pagadera por el Tesoro de los Estados Unidos. Mientras asistan a las sesiones de sus respectivas Cámaras, así como mientras se dirijan a ellas o regresen de las mismas, no podrán ser arrestados, excepto en casos de traición, delito grave o alteración de la paz. Tampoco podrán ser reconvenidos fuera de la Cámara por ninguno de sus discursos o por sus manifestaciones en cualquier debate en ella.

Ningún senador o representante, mientras dure el término por el cual fue elegido, será nombrado para ningún cargo civil bajo la autoridad de los Estados Unidos, que hubiere sido creado o cuyos emolumentos hubieren sido aumentados durante tal término; y nadie que desempeñe un cargo bajo la autoridad de los Estados Unidos podrá ser miembro de ninguna de las Cámaras mientras ocupe tal cargo.

SECCION 7. Todo proyecto de ley para imponer contribuciones se originará en la Cámara de Representantes; pero el Senado podrá proponer enmiendas o concurrir en ellas como en los demás proyectos.

Todo proyecto que hubiere sido aprobado por la Cámara de Representantes y el Senado será sometido al Presidente de los Estados Unidos antes de que se convierta en ley. Si el Presidente lo aprueba, lo firmará. De lo contrario, lo devolverá con sus objeciones a la Cámara en donde se originó el proyecto, la que insertará en su diario las objeciones íntegramente y procederá a reconsiderarlo. Si después de tal reconsideración dos terceras partes de dicha Cámara convinieren en aprobar el proyecto, éste se enviará, junto con las objeciones, a la otra Cámara, la que también lo reconsiderará y si resultare aprobado por las dos terceras partes de sus miembros, se convertirá en ley. En tales casos la votación en cada Cámara será nominal y los votos en pro y en contra del proyecto así como los nombres de los votantes se consignarán en el diario de cada una de ellas. Si el Presidente no devolviere un proyecto de ley dentro de los diez días (excluyendo los domingos), después de haberle sido presentado, dicho proyecto se convertirá en ley, tal cual si lo hubiere firmado, a no ser que, por haber recesado, el Congreso impida su devolución. En tal caso el proyecto no se convertirá en ley.

Toda orden, resolución o votación que requiera la concurrencia del Senado y de la Cámara de Representantes (salvo cuando se trate de levantar las sesiones) se presentará al Presidente de los Estados Unidos; y no tendrá efecto hasta que éste la apruebe o, en caso de ser desaprobada por él, hasta que dos terceras partes del Senado y de la Cámara de Representantes la aprueben nuevamente, conforme a las reglas y restricciones prescritas para los proyectos de ley.

SECCION 8. El Congreso tendrá facultad: para imponer y recaudar contribuciones, derechos, impuestos y arbitrios; para pagar las deudas y proveer para la defensa común y el bienestar general de los Estados Unidos; pero todos los derechos, impuestos y arbitrios serán uniformes en toda la Nación;

Para tomar dinero a préstamo con cargo al crédito de los Estados Unidos;

Para reglamentar el comercio con naciones extranjeras, así como entre los estados y con las tribus indias;

Para establecer una regla uniforme de naturalización y leyes uniformes de quiebras para toda la Nación;

Para acuñar moneda, reglamentar el valor de ésta y de la moneda extranjera, y fijar normas de pesas y medidas;

Para fijar penas por la falsificación de los valores y de la moneda de los Estados Unidos;

Para establecer oficinas de correo y vías postales;

Para fomentar el progreso de la ciencia y de las artes útiles, garantizando por tiempo limitado a los autores e inventores el derecho exclusivo a sus respectivos escritos y descubrimientos;

Para establecer tribunales inferiores al Tribunal Supremo;

Para definir y castigar la piratería y los delitos graves cometidos en alta mar, así como las infracciones del derecho internacional;

Para declarar la guerra, conceder patentes de corso y represalia y establecer reglas relativas a capturas en mar y tierra;

Para reclutar y mantener ejércitos; pero ninguna asignación para este fin lo será por un período mayor de dos años;

Para organizar y mantener una armada;

Para establecer reglas para el gobierno y reglamentación de la fuerzas de mar y tierra;

Para dictar reglas para llamar la milicia a fin de hacer cumplir las leyes de la Unión, sofocar insurrecciones y repeler invasiones;

Para proveer para la organización, armamento y disciplina de la milicia y el gobierno de aquella parte de ella que estuviere al servicio de los Estados Unidos, reservando a los estados respectivos el nombramiento de los oficiales y la autoridad para adiestrar a la milicia de acuerdo con la disciplina prescrita por el Congreso;

Para ejercer el derecho exclusivo a legislar en todas las materias concernientes a aquel distrito (cuya superficie no excederá de diez millas en cuadro) que, por cesión de algunos estados y aceptación del Congreso, se convirtiere en la sede del Gobierno de los Estados Unidos; y para ejercer igual autoridad sobre todas aquellas tierras adquiridas con el consentimiento de la Asamblea Legislativa del estado en que radicaren, con el fin de construir fuertes, almacenes, arsenales, astilleros y otras edificaciones que fueren necesarias; y

Para aprobar todas las leyes que fueren necesarias y convenientes para poner en práctica las precedentes facultades, así como todas aquellas que en virtud de esta Constitución puedan estar investidas en el Gobierno de los Estados Unidos o en cualquiera de sus departamentos o funcionarios.

SECCION 9. El Congreso no podrá antes del año 1808 prohibir la inmigración o importación de aquellas personas cuya admisión considere conveniente cualquiera de los estados existentes; pero se podrá imponer un tributo o impuesto a tal importación que no excederá de diez dólares por persona.

No se suspenderá el privilegio del auto de hábeas corpus, salvo cuando en casos de rebelión o invasión la seguridad pública así lo exija.

No se aprobará ningún proyecto para condenar sin celebración de juicio ni ninguna ley *ex post facto*.

No se impondrá capitación u otra contribución directa, sino en proporción al censo o enumeración que esta Constitución ordena se lleve a efecto.

No se impondrán contribuciones o impuestos sobre los artículos que se exporten de cualquier estado.

No se dará preferencia, por ningún reglamento de comercio o de rentas internas, a los puertos de un estado sobre los de otro. Tampoco podrá obligarse a las embarcaciones que se dirijan a un estado o salgan de él, que entren, descarguen o paguen impuestos en otro.

No se podrá retirar cantidad alguna del Tesoro sino a virtud de asignaciones hechas por ley; y periódicamente se publicará un estado completo de los ingresos y egresos públicos.

Los Estados Unidos no concederán títulos de nobleza; y ninguna persona que desempeñe bajo la autoridad del Gobierno un cargo retribuído o de confianza podrá aceptar, sin el consentimiento del Congreso, donativo, emolumento, empleo o título, de clase alguna, de ningún rey, príncipe o nación extranjera.

SECCION 10. Ningún estado celebrará tratado, alianza o confederación alguna; concederá patentes de corso y represalia; acuñará moneda; emitirá cartas de crédito; autorizará el pago de deudas en otro numerario que no sea oro y plata; aprobará ningún proyecto para condenar sin celebración de juicio, ley *ex post facto* o que menoscabe la obligación de los contratos, ni concederá títulos de nobleza.

Ningún estado podrá, sin el consentimiento del Congreso, fijar impuestos o derechos sobre las importaciones o exportaciones, salvo cuando fuere absolutamente necesario para hacer cumplir sus leyes de inspección; y el producto neto de todos los derechos e impuestos que fijare cualquier estado sobre las importaciones o exportaciones, ingresará en el Tesoro de los Estados Unidos. Todas esas leyes quedarán sujetas a la revisión e intervención del Congreso.

Ningún estado podrá, sin el consentimiento del Congreso, fijar derecho alguno de tonelaje, ni mantener tropas o embarcaciones de guerra en tiempos de paz, ni celebrar convenios o pactos con otro estado o con potencias extranjeras, ni entrar en guerra, a menos que fuere de hecho invadido o estuviere en peligro tan inminente que su defensa no admita demora.

ARTICULO II

SECCION 1. El poder ejecutivo residirá en el Presidente de los Estados Unidos de América. Este desempeñará sus funciones por un término de cuatro años y se le elegirá, junto con el vicepresidente, quien también desempeñará su cargo por un término similar, de la siguiente manera:

Cada estado designará, en la forma que prescribiere su Asamblea Legislativa, un número de compromisarios igual al número total de senadores y representantes que le corresponda en el Congreso; pero no será nombrado compromisario ningún senador o representante o persona alguna que ocupare un cargo de confianza o retribuído bajo la autoridad de los Estados Unidos.

Los compromisarios se reunirán en sus respectivos estados, y mediante votación secreta votarán por dos personas, de las cuales, por lo menos una no será residente del mismo estado que ellos. Se hará una lista de todas las personas por quienes se hubiere votado así como del número de votos que cada una obtuviere. Los compromisarios firmarán y certificarán esta lista, y la remitirán sellada a la sede del Gobierno de los Estados Unidos, dirigida al Presidente del Senado. En presencia del Senado y de la Cámara de Representantes, el Presidente del Senado abrirá todos los certificados y se procederá entonces a verificar el escrutinio. Será presidente la persona que obtuviere mayor número de votos si dicho número fuere la mayoría del número total de compromisarios designados. Si más de una persona obtuviere tal mayoría y recibiere el mismo número de votos, entonces de entre ellas la Cámara de Representantes, por votación secreta, elegirá inmediatamente al presidente. Si ninguna persona obtuviere mayoría, entonces la Cámara elegirá en igual forma al presidente de entre las cinco personas que hubieren obtenido más votos en la lista. Pero en la elección del presidente la votación será por estados y la representación de cada estado tendrá derecho a un voto. Para este fin el quórum constará de uno o más miembros de las dos terceras partes de las representaciones de los estados, y para que haya elección será necesaria una mayoría de todos los estados. En cualquier caso, una vez elegido el presidente, será vicepresidente la persona que obtuviere el mayor número de votos de los compromisarios. Pero si hubiere dos o más con un número igual de votos el Senado, por votación secreta, elegirá entre ellas al vicepresidente.

El Congreso determinará la fecha de seleccionar los compromisarios y el día en que habrán de votar, que serán los mismos en toda la Nación.

No será elegible para el cargo de presidente quien no fuere ciudadano por nacimiento o ciudadano de los Estados Unidos al tiempo en que se adopte esta Constitución. Tampoco lo será quien no hubiere cumplido treinta y cinco años de edad y no hubiere residido catorce años en los Estados Unidos.

En caso de destitución, muerte, renuncia o incapacidad del presidente para desempeñar las funciones de su cargo, le sustituirá el vicepresidente. En caso de destitución, muerte, renuncia o incapacidad tanto del presidente como del vicepresidente, el Congreso dispondrá mediante legislación quién desempeñará la presidencia y tal funcionario ejercerá el cargo hasta que cese la incapacidad o se elija un nuevo presidente.

Como remuneración por sus servicios el presidente recibirá, en las fechas que se determinen, una compensación que no podrá ser aumentada ni disminuída durante el término para el cual se le eligió, y no percibirá durante dicho término ningún otro emolumento de los Estados Unidos ni de ninguno de los estados.

Antes de comenzar a desempeñar su cargo, el presidente prestará el siguiente juramento o promesa: "Juro (o prometo) solemnemente que desempeñaré fielmente el cargo de Presidente de los Estados Unidos y que de la mejor manera a mi alcance guardaré, protegeré y defenderé la Constitución de los Estados Unidos."

SECCION 2. El presidente será jefe supremo del ejército y de la armada de los Estados Unidos, así como de la milicia de los distintos estados cuando ésta fuere llamada al servicio activo de la Nación. Podrá exigir opinión por escrito al jefe de cada departamento ejecutivo sobre cualquier asunto que se relacione con los deberes de sus respectivos cargos y tendrá facultad para suspender la ejecución de sentencias y para conceder indultos por delitos contra los Estados Unidos, salvo en casos de residencia.

Con el consejo y consentimiento del Senado tendrá poder para celebrar tratados, siempre que en ellos concurran las dos terceras partes de los senadores presentes. Asimismo, con el consejo y consentimiento del Senado, nombrará embajadores, otros ministros y cónsules públicos, los jueces del Tribunal Supremo y todos los demás funcionarios de los Estados Unidos cuyos cargos se establezcan por ley y cuyos nombramientos esta Constitución no prescriba. Pero el Congreso podrá por ley, confiar el nombramiento de aquellos funcionarios subalternos que creyere prudente, al presidente únicamente, a los tribunales de justicia o a los jefes de departamento.

El presidente tendrá poder para cubrir todas las vacantes que ocurrieren durante el receso del Senado, extendiendo nombramientos que expirarán al finalizar la próxima sesión del Senado.

SECCION 3. El presidente informará periódicamente al Congreso sobre el estado de la Unión y le recomendará aquellas medidas que él estime necesarias y convenientes. Podrá, en ocasiones extraordinarias, convocar a ambas Cámaras o a cualquiera de ellas; y en caso de que las Cámaras no estuvieren de acuerdo con relación a la fecha para recesar, el presidente podrá fijarla según lo juzgue conveniente. El presidente recibirá a los embajadores y demás ministros públicos. Velará por el fiel cumplimiento de las leyes y extenderá los nombramientos de todos los funcionarios de los Estados Unidos.

SECCION 4. El presidente, el vicepresidente y todos los funcionarios civiles de los Estados Unidos serán destituídos de sus cargos mediante procedimiento de residencia, previa acusación y convictos que fueren de traición, cohecho u otros delitos graves y menos graves.

ARTICULO III

SECCION 1. El poder judicial de los Estados Unidos residirá en un Tribunal Supremo y en aquellos tribunales inferiores que periódicamente el Congreso creare y estableciere. Los jueces, tanto del Tribunal Supremo como de tribunales inferiores, desempeñarán sus cargos mientras observen buena conducta y en determinadas fechas recibirán por sus servicios una compensación que no será rebajada mientras desempeñen sus cargos.

SECCION 2. El poder judicial se extenderá a todo caso que en derecho y equidad surja de esta Constitución, de las leyes de los Estados Unidos, así como de los tratados celebrados o que se celebraren bajo su autoridad; a todos los casos que afecten a embajadores y otros ministros y cónsules públicos; a todos los casos de almirantazgo y jurisdicción marítima; a todas las controversias en que los Estados Unidos sean parte; a las controversias entre dos o más estados; entre un estado y los ciudadanos de otro estado; entre los ciudadanos de diferentes estados; entre los ciudadanos del mismo estado que reclamaren tierras en virtud de concesiones hechas por diversos estados, y entre un estado o sus ciudadanos y estados, ciudadanos o súbditos extranjeros.

El Tribunal Supremo tendrá jurisdicción original en todos los casos que afectaren a embajadores, ministros y cónsules públicos y en aquellos en que un estado fuere parte. De todos los demás casos antes mencionados conocerá el Tribunal Supremo en apelación, tanto sobre cuestiones de derecho como de hecho, con las excepciones y bajo la reglamentación que el Congreso estableciere.

Se juzgarán ante jurado todas las causas criminales, excepto las que den lugar al procedimiento de residencia; y el juicio se celebrará en el estado en que se cometió el delito. Si no se cometiere en ningún estado, se celebrará el juicio en el sitio o en los sitios que el Congreso designare por ley.

SECCION 3. El delito de traición contra los Estados Unidos consistirá solamente en tomar las armas contra ellos o en unirse a sus enemigos, dándoles ayuda y facilidades. Nadie será convicto de traición sino por el testimonio de dos testigos del hecho incriminatorio o por confesión en corte abierta.

El Congreso tendrá poder para fijar la pena correspondiente al delito de traición; pero la sentencia por traición no alcanzará en sus efectos a los herederos del culpable ni llevará consigo la confiscación de sus bienes salvo durante la vida de la persona sentenciada.

ARTICULO IV

SECCION 1. Se dará entera fe y crédito en cada estado a los actos públicos, documentos y procedimientos judiciales de los otros estados. El Congreso podrá prescribir mediante leyes generales la manera de probar tales actos, documentos y procedimientos así como los efectos que deban surtir.

SECCION 2. Los ciudadanos de cada estado disfrutarán de todos los privilegios e inmunidades de los ciudadanos de otros estados.

Toda persona acusada de traición, delito grave o de cualquier otro delito, que huyere del estado en donde se le acusa y fuere hallada en otro estado, será, a solicitud de la autoridad ejecutiva del estado de donde se fugó, entregada a dicha autoridad para ser devuelta al estado que tuviere jurisdicción para conocer del delito.

Ninguna persona obligada a servir o trabajar en un estado, a tenor con las leyes allí vigentes, que huyere a otro estado, será dispensada de prestar dicho servicio o trabajo amparándose en leyes o reglamentos del estado al cual se acogiere, sino que será entregada a petición de la parte que tuviere derecho al susodicho servicio o trabajo.

SECCION 3. El Congreso podrá admitir nuevos estados a esta Unión; pero no se formará o establecerá ningún estado nuevo dentro de la jurisdicción de ningún otro estado. Tampoco se formará ningún estado por unión de dos o más estados, o partes de estados, sin el consentimiento tanto de las Asambleas Legislativas de los estados en cuestión como del Congreso.

El Congreso podrá disponer de, o promulgar todas las reglas y reglamentos necesarios en relación con, el territorio o cualquier propiedad perteneciente a los Estados Unidos. Ninguna disposición de esta Constitución se interpretará en forma tal que pudiere perjudicar cualesquiera reclamaciones de los Estados Unidos o de algún estado en particular.

SECCION 4. Los Estados Unidos garantizarán a cada estado de esta Unión una forma republicana de gobierno y protegerán a cada uno de ellos contra toda invasión; y cuando lo solicitare la Asamblea Legislativa o el Ejecutivo (si no se pudiere convocar la primera), le protegerá contra desórdenes internos.

ARTICULO V

El Congreso propondrá enmiendas a esta Constitución, siempre que dos terceras partes de ambas Cámaras lo estimen necesario; o, a petición de las Asambleas Legislativas de dos terceras partes de los estados, convocará una convención para proponer enmiendas, las cuales, en uno u otro caso, serán válidas para todos los fines y propósitos, como parte de esta Constitución, cuando las ratifiquen las Asambleas Legislativas de las tres cuartas partes de los estados, o las convenciones celebradas en las tres cuartas partes de los mismos, de acuerdo con el modo de ratificación propuesto por el Congreso; Disponiéndose, que ninguna enmienda hecha antes del año mil ochocientos ocho afectara en modo alguno los incisos primero y cuarto de la novena sección del primer artículo; y que no se privará a ningún estado, sin su consentimiento, de la igualdad de sufragio en el Senado.

ARTICULO VI

Todas las deudas y obligaciones contraídas antes de promulgarse esta Constitución serán tan válidas contra los Estados Unidos bajo esta Constitución como lo eran bajo la Confederación.

La presente Constitución, las leyes de los Estados Unidos que en virtud de ella se aprobaren y todos los tratados celebrados o que se celebraren bajo la autoridad de los Estados Unidos serán la suprema ley del país. Los jueces de cada estado estarán obligados a observarla aun cuando hubiere alguna disposición en contrario en la Constitución o en las leyes de cualquier estado.

Los senadores y representantes antes mencionados, los miembros de las Asambleas Legislativas de los diversos estados, así como todos los funcionarios ejecutivos y judiciales, tanto de los Estados Unidos como de los diversos estados, se comprometerán bajo juramento o promesa a sostener esta Constitución; pero no existirá requisito religioso alguno para desempeñar ningún cargo o empleo, retribuído o de confianza, bajo la autoridad de los Estados Unidos.

ARTICULO VII

La ratificación de las convenciones de nueve estados será suficiente para que esta Constitución rija entre los estados que la ratificaren.

DADA en convención con el consentimiento unánime de los estados presentes, el día diecisiete de septiembre del año de Nuestro Señor mil setecientos ochenta y siete, duodécimo de la independencia de los Estados Unidos de América. En testimonio de lo cual suscribimos la presente.

GEORGE WASHINGTON
Presidente y Diputado por Virgina

Doy fe: WILLIAM JACKSON, *Secretario*

Nueva Hampshire

JOHN LANGDON — NICHOLAS GILMAN

Massachusetts

NATHANIEL GORHAM — RUFUS KING

Connecticut

WM. SML. JOHNSON — ROGER SHERMAN

Nueva York

ALEXANDER HAMILTON

Nueva Jersey

WIL. LIVINGSTON — WM. PATERSON
DAVID BREARLEY — JONA. DAYTON

Pensilvania

B. FRANKLIN — THOS. FITZSIMONS
THOMAS MIFFLIN — JARED INGERSOLL

ROBT. MORRIS	JAMES WILSON
GEO. CLYMER	GOUV. MORRIS

Delaware

GEO. READ	RICHARD BASSETT
GUNNING BEDFORD (HIJO)	JACO. BROOM
JOHN DICKINSON	

Maryland

JAMES McHENRY	DANL. CARROLL
DAN. OF ST. THOS. JENIFER	

Virginia

JOHN BLAIR	JAMES MADISON (HIJO)

Carolina del Norte

WM. BLOUNT	HU. WILLIAMSON
RICH. DOBBS SPAIGHT	

Carolina del Sur

J. RUTLEDGE	CHARLES PINCKNEY
CHARLES COTESWORTH PINCKNEY	PIERCE BUTLER

Georgia

WILLIAM FEW	ABR. BALDWIN

ENMIENDAS

ENMIENDA I

El Congreso no aprobará ninguna ley con respecto al establecimiento de religión alguna, o que prohiba el libre ejercicio de la misma o que coarte la libertad de palabra o de prensa; o el derecho del pueblo a reunirse pacíficamente y a solicitar del Gobierno la reparación de agravios.

ENMIENDA II

Siendo necesaria para la seguridad de un Estado libre una milicia bien organizada, no se coartará el derecho del pueblo a tener y portar armas.

ENMIENDA III

En tiempos de paz ningún soldado será alojado en casa alguna, sin el consentimiento del propietario, ni tampoco lo será en tiempos de guerra sino de la manera prescrita por ley.

ENMIENDA IV

No se violará el derecho del pueblo a la seguridad de sus personas, hogares, documentos y pertenencias, contra registros y allanamientos irrazonables, y no se expedirá ningún mandamiento, sino a virtud de causa probable, apoyado por juramento o promesa, y que describa en detalle el lugar que ha de ser allanado, y las personas o cosas que han de ser detenidas o incautadas.

ENMIENDA V

Ninguna persona será obligada a responder por delito capital o infamante, sino en virtud de denuncia o acusación por un gran jurado, salvo en los casos que ocurran en las fuerzas de mar y tierra, o en la milicia, cuando se hallen en servicio activo en tiempos de guerra o de peligro público; ni podrá nadie ser sometido por el mismo delito dos veces a un juicio que pueda ocasionarle la pérdida de la vida o la integridad corporal; ni será compelido en ningún caso criminal a declarar contra sí mismo, ni será privado de su vida, de su libertad o de su propiedad, sin el debido procedimiento de ley; ni se podrá tomar propiedad privada para uso público, sin justa compensación.

ENMIENDA VI

En todas las causas criminales, el acusado gozará del derecho a un juicio rápido y público, ante un jurado imparcial del estado y distrito en que el delito haya sido cometido, distrito que será previamente fijado por ley; a ser informado de la naturaleza y causa de la acusación; a carearse con los testigos en su contra; a que se adopten medidas compulsivas para la comparecencia de los testigos que cite a su favor y a la asistencia de abogado para su defensa.

ENMIENDA VII

En litigios en derecho común, en que el valor en controversia exceda de veinte dólares, se mantendrá el derecho a juicio por jurado, y ningún hecho fallado por un jurado, será revisado por ningún tribunal de los Estados Unidos, sino de acuerdo con las reglas del derecho común.

ENMIENDA VIII

No se exigirán fianzas excesivas, ni se impondrán multas excesivas, ni castigos crueles e inusitados.

ENMIENDA IX

La inclusión de ciertos derechos en la Constitución no se interpretará en el sentido de denegar o restringir otros derechos que se haya reservado el pueblo.

ENMIENDA X

Las facultades que esta Constitución no delegue a los Estados Unidos, ni prohiba a los estados, quedan reservadas a los estados respectivamente o al pueblo.

ENMIENDA XI

El poder judicial de los Estados Unidos no será interpretado en el sentido de extenderse a los litigios en derecho o en equidad, incoados o seguidos contra uno de los estados de la Unión por ciudadanos de otro estado, o por ciudadanos o súbditos de cualquier estado extranjero.

ENMIENDA XII

Los compromisarios se reunirán en sus respectivos estados y votarán por votación secreta para presidente y vicepresidente, uno de los cuales, por lo menos, no será residente del mismo estado que ellos; designarán en sus papeletas la persona votada para presidente, y en papeleta distinta la persona votada para vicepresidente, y harán listas distintas de todas las personas votadas para presidente, y de todas las personas votadas para vicepresidente, con indicación del número de votos emitidos en favor de cada una, listas que serán firmadas y certificadas y remitidas por ellos debidamente selladas a la sede del gobierno de los Estados Unidos, dirigidas al Presidente del Senado. Este, en presencia del Senado y de la Cámara de Representantes, abrirá todos los certificados y se procederá a contar los votos. La persona que obtenga el mayor número de votos para el cargo de presidente, será presidente, si tal número constituye la mayoría del número total de los compromisarios nombrados; y si ninguna persona obtuviese tal mayoría, entonces de entre las tres personas que obtengan el mayor número de votos para presidente, la Cámara de Representantes elegirá inmediatamente, por votación secreta, al presidente. Pero al elegir al presidente, los votos se emitirán por estados, teniendo un voto la representación de cada estado; a este fin, el quorum consistirá de un miembro o miembros de dos terceras partes de los estados, siendo necesaria la mayoría de todos los estados para la elección. Y si la Cámara de Representantes, cuando el derecho de elegir recaiga sobre ella, no elige presidente antes del cuarto día del mes de marzo siguiente, entonces el vicepresidente actuará como presidente, al igual que en el caso de muerte u otra incapacidad constitucional del presidente. Será vicepresidente la persona que obtenga el mayor número de votos para el cargo de vicepresidente, si dicho número equivale a la mayoría del número total de compromisarios designados. Si ninguna persona obtiene mayoría, entonces el Senado elegirá al vicepresidente de entre las dos personas que obtengan el mayor número de votos. A este fin el quorum consistirá de las dos terceras partes del número total de senadores, requiriéndose la mayoría del número total para la elección. Ninguna persona inelegible constitucionalmente para el cargo de presidente será elegible para el de vicepresidente de los Estados Unidos.

ENMIENDA XIII

SECCION 1. Ni la esclavitud ni la servidumbre involuntaria existirán en los Estados Unidos o en cualquier lugar sujeto a su jurisdicción, salvo como castigo por un delito del cual la persona haya sido debidamente convicta.

SECCION 2. El Congreso tendrá facultad para hacer cumplir las disposiciones de esta enmienda mediante legislación adecuada.

ENMIENDA XIV

SECCION 1. Toda persona nacida o naturalizada en los Estados Unidos y sujeta a su jurisdicción, será ciudadana de los Estados Unidos y del estado en que resida. Ningún estado aprobará o hará cumplir ninguna ley que restrinja los privilegios o inmunidades de los ciudadanos de los Estados Unidos; ni ningún estado privará a persona alguna de su vida, de su libertad o de su propiedad, sin el debido procedimiento de ley, ni negará a nadie, dentro de su jurisdicción, la igual protección de las leyes.

SECCION 2. Los representantes serán prorrateados entre los diversos estados de conformidad con sus respectivos habitantes, contando el número total de personas en cada estado, excluyendo a los indios que no paguen contribuciones. Pero cuando en cualquier elección para la designación de compromisarios que hayan de elegir al presidente y al vicepresidente de los Estados Unidos, a los representantes en el Congreso, a los funcionarios ejecutivos y judiciales de un estado o a los miembros de su Asamblea Legislativa, se negare el derecho a votar a cualquiera de los residentes varones de tal estado que tenga veintiún años de edad y sea ciudadano de los Estados Unidos, o cuando de cualquier modo ese derecho le sea restringido, excepto por participar en cualquier rebelión o en otro delito, la base de la representación será reducida en dicho estado en la proporción que el número de tales ciudadanos varones guarde con respecto al total de ciudadanos varones de veintiún años de edad en tal estado.

SECCION 3. No será senador o representante en el Congreso, ni compromisario para elegir presidente o vicepresidente, ni desempeñará cargo civil o militar alguno, bajo la autoridad de los Estados Unidos o de cualquier estado, quien, habiendo jurado previamente defender la Constitución de los Estados Unidos, como miembro del Congreso, como funcionario de los Estados Unidos o como miembro de una Asamblea Legislativa de cualquier estado o como funcionario ejecutivo o judicial del mismo, haya tomado parte en alguna insurrección o rebelión contra los Estados Unidos, o haya suministrado ayuda o facilidades a sus enemigos. Pero el Congreso, por el voto de dos terceras partes de cada Cámara, podrá dispensar tal incapacidad.

SECCION 4. No se cuestionará la validez de la deuda pública de los Estados Unidos autorizada por ley, incluyendo las deudas contraídas para el pago de pensiones y recompensas por servicios prestados para sofocar insurrecciones o rebeliones. Pero ni los Estados Unidos ni ningún estado asumirá o pagará deuda u obligación alguna contraída en ayuda de insurrección o rebelión contra los Estados Unidos, ni reclamación alguna por la pérdida o emancipación de ningún esclavo; y tales deudas, obligaciones y reclamaciones serán consideradas ilegales y nulas.

SECCION 5. El Congreso tendrá facultad para hacer cumplir las disposiciones de esta enmienda mediante legislación adecuada.

ENMIENDA XV

SECCION 1. Ni los Estados Unidos ni ningún estado de la Unión negará o coartará a los ciudadanos de los Estados Unidos el derecho al sufragio por razón de raza, color o condición previa de esclavitud.

SECCION 2. El Congreso tendrá facultad para hacer cumplir las disposiciones de esta enmienda mediante legislación adecuada.

ENMIENDA XVI

El Congreso tendrá facultad para imponer y recaudar contribuciones sobre ingresos, sea cual fuere la fuente de que se deriven, sin prorrateo entre los diversos estados y sin considerar ningún censo o enumeración.

ENMIENDA XVII

El Senado de los Estados Unidos se compondrá de dos senadores por cada estado, elegidos por el pueblo de éste por un período de seis años, y cada senador tendrá derecho a un voto. Los electores de cada estado deberán poseer los requisitos necesarios para ser electores de la rama más numerosa de las Asambleas legislativas estatales.

Cuando en el Senado ocurran vacantes en la representación de algún estado, la autoridad ejecutiva de tal estado convocará a elecciones para cubrir tales vacantes, disponiéndose que la Asamblea Legislativa de cualquier estado podrá facultar a su ejecutivo a extender nombramientos provisionales hasta que el pueblo cubra las vacantes por elección, en la forma que disponga la Asamblea Legislativa.

Esta enmienda no será interpretada en el sentido de afectar la elección o término de ningún senador elegido antes de que se convalide la misma como parte de la Constitución.

ENMIENDA XVIII

SECCION 1. Transcurrido un año después de la ratificación de esta enmienda, quedan prohibidas la fabricación, venta o transportación dentro de, así como la importación a o la exportación desde los Estados Unidos y todo territorio sujeto a su jurisdicción, de bebidas embriagantes.

SECCION 2. El Congreso y los diversos Estados tendrán facultad concurrente para hacer cumplir las disposiciones de esta enmienda mediante legislación adecuada.

SECCION 3. Esta enmienda no surtirá efecto alguno a menos que las Asambleas Legislativas de los diversos estados la ratifiquen como enmienda a la Constitución, conforme a lo preceptuado en ésta, dentro de siete años contados a partir de la fecha en que el Congreso la someta a la consideración de los estados.

ENMIENDA XIX

El derecho de sufragio de los ciudadanos de los Estados Unidos no será negado o coartado por los Estados Unidos o por ningún estado por razón de sexo.

El Congreso tendrá facultad para hacer cumplir las disposiciones de esta enmienda mediante legislación adecuada.

ENMIENDA XX

SECCION 1. El término del presidente y del vicepresidente expirará al mediodía del vigésimo día de enero, y el de los senadores y representantes al mediodía del tercer día de enero, de los años en los cuales tal término hubiese expirado de no haberse ratificado esta enmienda; y entonces empezará el término de sus sucesores.

SECCION 2. El Congreso se reunirá por lo menos una vez al año y tal sesión comenzará al mediodía del tercer día de enero, a menos que por ley se fije otra fecha.

SECCION 3. Si en la fecha en que el presidente haya de empezar a desempeñar su cargo, el presidente electo hubiere muerto, el vicepresidente electo será el presidente. Si no se hubiere elegido presidente antes de la fecha en que debe empezar a desempeñar su cargo, o si el presidente electo dejare de tomar posesión, entonces el vicepresidente electo actuará como presidente hasta que un presidente quede habilitado; y el Congreso podrá por ley proveer para el caso en que ni el presidente ni el vicepresidente electos reúnan los requisitos necesarios, declarando quién actuará entonces como presidente, o el modo en que se seleccionará el que haya de actuar como tal, debiendo dicha persona actuar en esa capacidad hasta que se designe un presidente o un vicepresidente que reúna los requisitos necesarios.

SECCION 4. El Congreso podrá por ley proveer para el caso del fallecimiento de cualquiera de las personas de entre las cuales la Cámara de Representantes puede elegir un presidente, cuando sobre ella recaiga el derecho de tal eleción, y para el caso del fallecimiento de cualquiera de las personas de entre las cuales el Senado puede elegir un vicepresidente, cuando sobre dicho Senado recaiga el derecho de tal elección.

SECCION 5. Las secciones 1 y 2 empezarán a regir el décimoquinto día del mes de octubre siguiente a la ratificación de esta enmienda.

SECCION 6. Esta enmienda no surtirá efecto alguno a menos que las Asambleas Legislativas de tres cuartas partes de los diversos estados la ratifiquen como enmienda a la Constitución, dentro de siete años contados a partir de la fecha en que les sea sometida.

ENMIENDA XXI

SECCION 1. La Enmienda XVIII a la Constitución de los Estados Unidos queda por la presente derogada.

SECCION 2. La transportación o importación de bebidas embriagantes a cualquier estado, territorio o posesión de los Estados Unidos, para entrega o uso en los mismos, en violación de las leyes allí en vigor, queda por la presente prohibida.

SECCION 3. Esta enmienda no surtirá efecto alguno a menos que haya sido ratificada como enmienda a la Constitución por convenciones en los diversos estados, conforme a lo preceptuado en la Constitución, dentro de siete años contados a partir de la fecha en que el Congreso la someta a la consideración de los estados.

ENMIENDA XXII

Nadie podrá ser elegido más de dos veces para el cargo de presidente, y nadie que haya ocupado el cargo de presidente, o que haya actuado como presidente por más de dos años del término para el cual fue elegida otra persona, podrá ser elegido más de una vez para el cargo de presidente. Pero este artículo no se aplicará a persona alguna que ocupara el cargo de presidente cuando dicho artículo fue propuesto por el Congreso, y no impedirá que cualquier persona que esté ocupando el cargo de presidente, o actuando como presidente, durante el término en que este artículo entre en vigor, ocupe el cargo de presidente o actúe como presidente durante el resto de dicho término.

Este Articulo se quedará inoperativo a menos que sea ratificado como enmienda a la Constitución por las legislaturas de tres cuatros de los varios Estados dentro de 7 anos después de la fecha de su presentación a los Estados por el Congreso.

ENMIENDA XXIII

SECCION 1. Por constituir la sede del Gobierno de los Estados Unidos, el Distrito nombrará en la forma que los disponga el Congreso:

Un número de compromisarios de presidente y vicepresidente que será igual al número total de senadores y representantes en el Congreso a que el Distrito tendría derecho si fuera un estado, pero en ningún caso mayor que el número de compromisarios del estado menos poblado; dichos compromisarios se nombrarán además de los elegidos por los estados, pero se considerarán, para los fines de la elección de presidente y vicepresidente, como compromisarios nombrados por un estado; y se reunirán en el Distrito y realizarán las funciones prescritas por la duodécima enmienda.

SECCION 2. El Congreso tendrá facultad para hacer cumplir las disposiciones de este artículo mediante legislación adecuada.

ENMIENDA XXIV

SECCION 1. El derecho que tienen los ciudadanos de los Estados Unidos de votar en cualquier elección primaria, o de otra naturaleza, de presidente o vicepresidente de compromisarios de presidente o vicepresidente, o de senador o representante en el Congreso, no les será negado o restringido por los Estados Unidos o por cualquier estado por razones de falta de pago de cualquier impuesto de capitación o de otra naturaleza.

SECCION 2. El Congreso tendrá facultad para hacer cumplir las disposiciones de este artículo mediante legislación adecuada.

ENMIENDA XXV

SECCION 1. En caso de destitución, muerte o renuncia del presidente, el vicepresidente reemplazará al presidente.

SECCION 2. Cuando ocurra una vacante en el cargo de vicepresidente, el presidente designará un vicepresidente, quien tomará posesión de su cargo una vez que ambas Cámaras del Congreso confirmen su designación por mayoría de votos.

SECCION 3. Cuando el presidente trasmita al presidente pro témpore del Senado y al presidente de la Cámara de Representantes su declaración por escrito de que se encuentra imposibilitado para desempeñar los deberes y atribuciones de su cargo, y mientras no les envíe por escrito una declaración en contrario, tales deberes y atribuciones serán desempeñadas por el vicepresidente con el carácter de presidente interino.

SECCION 4. Cuando el vicepresidente y la mayoría de cualesquiera de los principales funcionarios de los departamentos ejecutivos, o de otros cuerpos que el Congreso establezca por ley, trasmitan al presidente pro témpore del Senado y al presidente de la Cámara de Representantes su declaración por escrito de que el presidente se encuentra imposibilitado para desempeñar los deberes y atribuciones de su cargo, el vicepresidente asumirá inmediatamente los deberes y atribuciones del cargo con el carácter de presidente interino.

En lo sucesivo, cuando el presidente trasmita al presidente pro témpore del Senado y al presidente de la Cámara de Representantes su declaración por escrito de que no existe incapacidad, el presidente reanudará los deberes y atribuciones de su cargo, a menos que el vicepresidente y la mayoría de cualesquiera de los principales funcionarios del departamento ejecutivo o de otros cuerpos que el Congreso establezca por ley, trasmitan al presidente pro témpore del Senado y al presidente de la Cámara de Representantes, dentro del plazo de cuatro días, su declaración por escrito de que el presidente se encuentra imposibilitado para desempeñar los deberes y atribuciones de su cargo. Entonces el Congreso decidirá el asunto, reuniéndose para ese objeto dentro del término de cuarenta y ocho horas, si no está en período de sesiones. Si el Congreso, dentro de los veintiún días posteriores al recibo de esta última declaración por escrito, o dentro de veintiún días de la fecha en que deba reunirse si el Congreso no está en período de sesiones, determina, por voto de los dos tercios de ambas Cámaras, que el presidente está imposibilitado para desempeñar los deberes y atribuciones de su cargo, el vicepresidente continuará desempeñándolas con el carácter de presidente interino; si no, el presidente reanudará el desempeño de los deberes y atribuciones de su cargo.

ENMIENDA XXVI

El derecho al voto que tienen los ciudadanos de los Estados Unidos que tengan 18 o más años de edad no les será negado o restringido por los Estados Unidos o por cualquier estado por razón de su edad.

Ejemplos de los Formularios Que Usted Deberá Completar

FEDERAL BUREAU OF INVESTIGATION
UNITED STATES DEPARTMENT OF JUSTICE
WASHINGTON, D.C. 20537

APPLICANT

1. LOOP

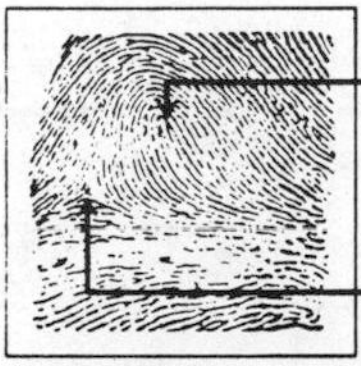

CENTER OF LOOP

DELTA

THE LINES BETWEEN CENTER OF LOOP AND DELTA MUST SHOW

2. WHORL

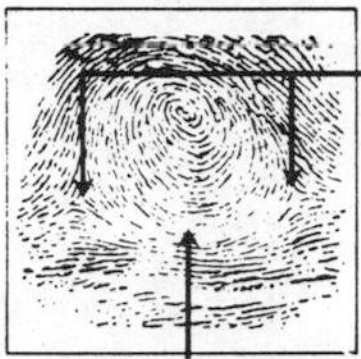

DELTAS

THESE LINES RUNNING BETWEEN DELTAS MUST BE CLEAR

3. ARCH

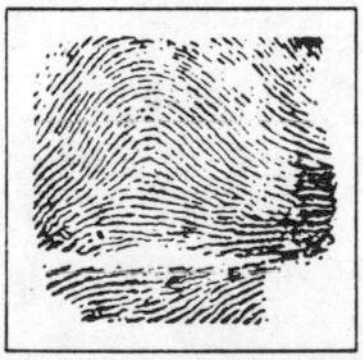

ARCHES HAVE NO DELTAS

TO OBTAIN CLASSIFIABLE FINGERPRINTS

1. USE BLACK PRINTER'S INK.
2. DISTRIBUTE INK EVENLY ON INKING SLAB.
3. WASH AND DRY FINGERS THOROUGHLY.
4. ROLL FINGERS FROM NAIL TO NAIL, AND AVOID ALLOWING FINGERS TO SLIP.
5. BE SURE IMPRESSIONS ARE RECORDED IN CORRECT ORDER.
6. IF AN AMPUTATION OR DEFORMITY MAKES IT IMPOSSIBLE TO PRINT A FINGER, MAKE A NOTATION TO THAT EFFECT IN THE INDIVIDUAL FINGER BLOCK.
7. IF SOME PHYSICAL CONDITION MAKES IT IMPOSSIBLE TO OBTAIN PERFECT IMPRESSIONS, SUBMIT THE BEST THAT CAN BE OBTAINED WITH A MEMO STAPLED TO THE CARD EXPLAINING THE CIRCUMSTANCES.
8. EXAMINE THE COMPLETED PRINTS TO SEE IF THEY CAN BE CLASSIFIED, BEARING IN MIND THAT MOST FINGERPRINTS FALL INTO THE PATTERNS SHOWN ON THIS CARD (OTHER PATTERNS OCCUR INFREQUENTLY AND ARE NOT SHOWN HERE).

THIS CARD FOR USE BY:

1. LAW ENFORCEMENT AGENCIES IN FINGERPRINTING APPLICANTS FOR LAW ENFORCEMENT POSITIONS.*
2. OFFICIALS OF STATE AND LOCAL GOVERNMENTS FOR PURPOSES OF EMPLOYMENT, LICENSING, AND PERMITS, AS AUTHORIZED BY STATE STATUTES AND APPROVED BY THE ATTORNEY GENERAL OF THE UNITED STATES. LOCAL AND COUNTY ORDINANCES, UNLESS SPECIFICALLY BASED ON APPLICABLE STATE STATUTES DO NOT SATISFY THIS REQUIREMENT.*
3. U.S. GOVERNMENT AGENCIES AND OTHER ENTITIES REQUIRED BY FEDERAL LAW.**
4. OFFICIALS OF FEDERALLY CHARTERED OR INSURED BANKING INSTITUTIONS TO PROMOTE OR MAINTAIN THE SECURITY OF THOSE INSTITUTIONS.

LEAVE THIS SPACE BLANK

INSTRUCTIONS:

*1. PRINTS MUST FIRST BE CHECKED THROUGH THE APPROPRIATE STATE IDENTIFICATION BUREAU, AND ONLY THOSE FINGERPRINTS FOR WHICH NO DISQUALIFYING RECORD HAS BEEN FOUND LOCALLY SHOULD BE SUBMITTED FOR FBI SEARCH.

2. PRIVACY ACT OF 1974 (P.L. 93-579) REQUIRES THAT FEDERAL, STATE, OR LOCAL AGENCIES INFORM INDIVIDUALS WHOSE SOCIAL SECURITY NUMBER IS REQUESTED WHETHER SUCH DISCLOSURE IS MANDATORY OR VOLUNTARY, BASIS OF AUTHORITY FOR SUCH SOLICITATION, AND USES WHICH WILL BE MADE OF IT.

**3. IDENTITY OF PRIVATE CONTRACTORS SHOULD BE SHOWN IN SPACE "EMPLOYER AND ADDRESS". THE CONTRIBUTOR IS THE NAME OF THE AGENCY SUBMITTING THE FINGERPRINT CARD TO THE FBI.

4. FBI NUMBER, IF KNOWN, SHOULD ALWAYS BE FURNISHED IN THE APPROPRIATE SPACE.

MISCELLANEOUS NO. – RECORD: OTHER ARMED FORCES NO., PASSPORT NO. (PP), ALIEN REGISTRATION NO. (AR), PORT SECURITY CARD NO. (PS), SELECTIVE SERVICE NO. (SS), VETERANS' ADMINISTRATION CLAIM NO. (VA.).

FD-258 (REV. 7-13-77)

☆ U.S. GOVERNMENT PRINTING OFFICE : 1980 – 317-188

Tarjeta de Huellas Digitales

APPLICANT

LEAVE BLANK

TYPE OR PRINT ALL INFORMATION IN BLACK

LAST NAME NAM | FIRST NAME | MIDDLE NAME

FBI | LEAVE BLANK

SIGNATURE OF PERSON FINGERPRINTED

ALIASES AKA

ORI NYINSNYOO
USINS
NEW YORK, NY

RESIDENCE OF PERSON FINGERPRINTED

DATE OF BIRTH DOB (Month, Day, Year)

CITIZENSHIP CTZ | SEX | RACE | HGT. | WGT. | EYES | HAIR | PLACE OF BIRTH POB

DATE | SIGNATURE OF OFFICIAL TAKING FINGERPRINTS

YOUR NO. OCA

LEAVE BLANK

EMPLOYER AND ADDRESS

FBI NO. FBI

CLASS

ARMED FORCES NO. MNU

REASON FINGERPRINTED

SOCIAL SECURITY NO. SOC

REF.

MISCELLANEOUS NO. MNU

1. R. THUMB	2. R. INDEX	3. R. MIDDLE	4. R. RING	5. R. LITTLE
6. L. THUMB	7. L. INDEX	8. L. MIDDLE	9. L. RING	10. L. LITTLE

LEFT FOUR FINGERS TAKEN SIMULTANEOUSLY | L. THUMB | R. THUMB | RIGHT FOUR FINGERS TAKEN SIMULTANEOUSLY

Tarjeta de Huellas Digitales

(Please tear off this sheet before submitting Affidavit)

U. S. Department of Justice
Immigration and Naturalization Service

Affidavit of Support

INSTRUCTIONS

I. EXECUTION OF AFFIDAVIT. A separate affidavit must be submitted for each person. You must sign the affidavit in your full, true and correct name and affirm or make it under oath. If you are **in the United States** the affidavit may be sworn or affirmed before an immigration officer without the payment of fee, or before a notary public or other officer authorized to administer oaths for general purposes, in which case the official seal or certificate of authority to administer oaths must be affixed. If you are **outside the United States** the affidavit must be sworn to or affirmed before a United States consular or immigration officer.

II. SUPPORTING EVIDENCE. The deponent must submit in duplicate evidence of income and resources, as appropriate:

A. Statement from an officer of the bank or other financial institution in which you have deposits giving the following details regarding your account:

1. Date account opened.
2. Total amount deposited for the past year.
3. Present balance.

B. Statement of your employer on business stationery, showing:

1. Date and nature of employment.
2. Salary paid.
3. Whether position is temporary or permanent.

C. If self-employed:

1. Copy of last income tax return filed or,
2. Report of commercial rating concern.

D. List containing serial numbers and denominations of bonds and name of record owner(s).

III. SPONSOR AND ALIEN LIABILITY. Effective October 1, 1980, amendments to section 1614(f) of the Social Security Act and Part A of Title XVI of the Social Security Act establish certain requirements for determining the eligibility of aliens who apply for the first time for Supplemental Security Income (SSI) benefits. Effective October 1, 1981, amendments to section 415 of the Social Security Act establish similar requirements for determining the eligibility of aliens who apply for the first time for Aid to Families with Dependent Children (AFDC) benefits. Effective December 22, 1981, amendments to the Food Stamp Act of 1977 affect the eligibility of alien participation in the Food Stamp Program. These amendments require that the income and resources of any person who, as the sponsor of an alien's entry into the United States, executes an affidavit of support or similar agreement on behalf of the alien, and the income and resources of the sponsor's spouse (*if living with the sponsor*) shall be deemed to be the income and resources of the alien under formulas for determining eligibility for SSI, AFDC, and Food Stamp benefits during the three years following the alien's entry into the United States.

An alien applying for SSI must make available to the Social Security Administration documentation concerning his or her income and resources and those of the sponsor including information which was provided in support of the application for an immigrant visa or adjustment of status. An alien applying for AFDC or Food Stamps must make similar information available to the State public assistance agency. The Secretary of Health and Human Services and the Secretary of Agriculture are authorized to obtain copies of any such documentation submitted to INS or the Department of State and to release such documentation to a State public assistance agency.

Sections 1621(e) and 415(d) of the Social Security Act and subsection 5(i) of the Food Stamp Act also provide that an alien and his or her sponsor shall be jointly and severably liable to repay any SSI, AFDC, or Food Stamp benefits which are incorrectly paid because of misinformation provided by a sponsor or because of a sponsor's failure to provide information. Incorrect payments which are not repaid will be withheld from any subsequent payments for which the alien or sponsor are otherwise eligible under the Social Security Act or Food Stamp Act, except that the sponsor was without fault or where good cause existed.

These provisions do not apply to the SSI, AFDC or Food Stamp eligibility of aliens admitted as refugees, granted political asylum by the Attorney General, or Cuban/Haitian entrants as defined in section 501(e) of P.L. 96-422 and of dependent children of the sponsor or sponsor's spouse. They also do not apply to the SSI or Food Stamp eligibility of an alien who becomes blind or disabled after admission into the United States for permanent residency.

IV. AUTHORITY/USE/PENALTIES. Authority for the collection of the information requested on this form is contained in 8 U.S.C. 1182(a)(15), 1184(a), and 1258. The information will be used principally by the Service, or by any consular officer to whom it may be furnished, to support an alien's application for benefits under the Immigration and Nationality Act and specifically the assertion that he or she has adequate means of financial support and will not become a public charge. Submission of the information is voluntary. It may also, as a matter of routine use, be disclosed to other federal, state, local and foreign law enforcement and regulatory agencies, including the Department of Health and Human Services, the Department of Agriculture, the Department of State, the Department of Defense and any component thereof (if the deponent has served or is serving in the armed forces of the United States), the Central Intelligence Agency, and individuals and organizations during the course of any investigation to elicit further information required to carry out Service functions. Failure to provide the information may result in the denial of the alien's application for a visa, or his or her exclusion from the United States.

OMB No. 1115-0062

U. S. Department of Justice
Immigration and Naturalization Service

Affidavit of Support

(ANSWER ALL ITEMS: FILL IN WITH TYPEWRITER OR PRINT IN BLOCK LETTERS IN INK.)

I, ______________________ (Name), ***residing at*** ______________________ (Street and Number)

______________________ (City) (State) (ZIP Code if in U.S.) (Country)

BEING DULY SWORN DEPOSE AND SAY:

1. I was born on ______________ (Date) at ______________ (City) (Country)

   If you are ***not*** a native born United States citizen, answer the following as appropriate:

   a. If a United States citizen through naturalization, give certificate of naturalization number ______________

   b. If a United States citizen through parent(s) or marriage, give citizenship certificate number ______________

   c. If United States citizenship was derived by some other method, attach a statement of explanation.

   d. If a lawfully admitted permanent resident of the United States, give "A" number ______________

2. That I am ______ years of age and have resided in the United States since (date) ______________
3. That this affidavit is executed in behalf of the following person:

Name			Sex	Age
Citizen of--(Country)	Marital Status	Relationship to Deponent		
Presently resides at--(Street and Number)	(City)	(State)	(Country)	

Name of spouse and children accompanying or following to join person:

Spouse	Sex	Age	Child	Sex	Age
Child	Sex	Age	Child	Sex	Age
Child	Sex	Age	Child	Sex	Age

4. That this affidavit is made by me for the purpose of assuring the United States Government that the person(s) named in item 3 will not become a public charge in the United States.

5. That I am willing and able to receive, maintain and support the person(s) named in item 3. That I am ready and willing to deposit a bond, if necessary, to guarantee that such person(s) will not become a public charge during his or her stay in the United States, or to guarantee that the above named will maintain his or her nonimmigrant status if admitted temporarily and will depart prior to the expiration of his or her authorized stay in the United States.

6. That I understand this affidavit will be binding upon me for a period of three (3) years after entry of the person(s) named in item 3 and that the information and documentation provided by me may be made available to the Secretary of Health and Human Services and the Secretary of Agriculture, who may make it available to a public assistance agency.

7. That I am employed as, or engaged in the business of ______________ (Type of Business) with ______________ (Name of concern)

   at ______________ (Street and Number) (City) (State) (Zip Code)

   I derive an annual income of *(if self-employed, I have attached a copy of my last income tax return or report of commercial rating concern which I certify to be true and correct to the best of my knowledge and belief. See instruction for nature of evidence of net worth to be submitted.)* $______________

   I have on deposit in savings banks in the United States $______________

   I have other personal property, the reasonable value of which is $______________

I have stocks and bonds with the following market value, as indicated on the attached list which I certify to be true and correct to the best of my knowledge and belief. **$ ____________**
I have life insurance in the sum of **$ ____________**
With a cash surrender value of **$ ____________**
I own real estate valued at **$ ____________**
With mortgages or other encumbrances thereon amounting to $ ____________

Which is located at ____
(Street and Number) (City) (State) (Zip Code)

8. That the following persons are dependent upon me for support: *(Place an "X" in the appropriate column to indicate whether the person named is* ***wholly*** *or* ***partially*** *dependent upon you for support.)*

Name of Person	Wholly Dependent	Partially Dependent	Age	Relationship to Me

9. That I have previously submitted affidavit(s) of support for the following person(s). If none, state ***"None"***

Name	Date submitted

10. That I have submitted visa petition(s) to the Immigration and Naturalization Service on behalf of the following person(s). If none, state none.

Name	Relationship	Date submitted

11. ***(Complete this block only if the person named in item 3 will be in the United States temporarily.)***
That I ☐ do intend ☐ do not intend, to make specific contributions to the support of the person named in item 3. *(If you check "do intend", indicate the exact nature and duration of the contributions. For example, if you intend to furnish room and board, state for how long and, if money, state the amount in United States dollars and state whether it is to be given in a lump sum, weekly, or monthly, or for how long.)*

____

____

____

OATH OR AFFIRMATION OF DEPONENT

I acknowledge at that I have read Part III of the Instructions, Sponsor and Alien Liability, and am aware of my responsibilities as an immigrant sponsor under the Social Security Act, as amended, and the Food Stamp Act, as amended.

I swear (affirm) that I know the contents of this affidavit signed by me and the statements are true and correct.

Signature of deponent ______________________________

Subscribed and sworn to (affirmed) before me this ________ ***day of*** ____________________, 19______

at ______________________________ ***.My commission expires on*** ____________________

Signature of Officer Administering Oath ______________________ ***Title*** ____________

If affidavit prepared by other than deponent, please complete the following: I declare that this document was prepared by me at the request of the deponent and is based on all information of which I have knowledge.

____

(Signature) ***(Address)*** ***(Date)***

U.S. Department of Justice
Immigration and Naturalization Service (INS)

Application for Permanent Residence

Instructions

Read the instructions carefully. If you do not follow the instructions, we may have to return your application, which may delay final action.

You will be required to appear before an Immigration Officer to answer questions about this application. You must bring your temporary entry permit (Form I-94, Arrival Departure Record) and your passport to your interview.

1. Who can apply?

You are eligible to apply for lawful permanent residence if you are in the U.S. and you:

A. have an immigrant visa number immediately available to you (see 3 below - "When will a visa become available?"), or

B. entered with a fiance(e) visa and have married within ninety days, or

C. have been granted asylum by the INS or an immigration judge one year or more ago, or

D. are a member of a class of "special immigrants", which includes certain immigrants returning from a temporary visit abroad, certain ministers of religion, and certain former employees of the United States abroad, or

E. have resided continuously in the United States since before June 30, 1948, or

F. are filing a motion before an immigration judge, or

G. are a former foreign government official, or a member of the immediate family of that official.

2. Who may not apply?

You are not eligible for lawful permanent residence if you entered the United States and you:

A. were not inspected and admitted or paroled by a United States Immigration Officer, or

B. continued in or accepted unauthorized employment, on or after January 1, 1977, unless you are the spouse, parent, or child of a United States citizen, or

C. are an exchange visitor subject to the two-year foreign residence requirement, or

D. were in transit through the United States without a visa, or

E. were admitted as a crewman of either a vessel or an aircraft.

NOTE: If you are included under 2 above but have lived here continuously since before June 30, 1948, you may still apply.

3. When will a visa become available?

If you are applying for permanent residence as the relative of a U.S. citizen or lawful permanent resident, or as an immigrant employee, an immigrant visa petition (I-130 or I-140) must have been filed (or must be filed with your application). In addition, an immigrant visa number must be immediately available to you.

If you are the husband, wife, parent, or minor unmarried child of a U.S. citizen, a visa is immediately available to you when your U.S. citizen relative's petition, Form I-130, for you is approved.

For all other applicants, the availability of visa numbers is based on priority dates, which are determined by the filing of immigrant visa applications or labor certifications. When the priority date is reached for your approved petition, a visa number is immediately available to you. For a monthly update of the dates for which visa numbers are available, you may call (202) 632-2919.

4. What documents do you need?

A. 1) For each document needed, give INS the original and one copy. **Originals will be returned to you**.

2) If you do not wish to give INS an original document, you may give INS a copy. The copy must be certified by:

a) an INS or U.S. consular officer, or

b) an attorney admitted to practice law in the United States, or

c) an INS accredited representative

(INS still may require originals).

3) Documents in a foreign language must be accompanied by a complete English translation. The translator must certify that the translation is accurate and that he or she is competent to translate.

B. You must also give INS the following documents:

1) Your birth certificate.

2) If you are between 14 and 70 years of age, Form G-325A (Biographic Information).

3) a) If you are employed, a letter from your present employer showing that you have employment of a permanent nature.

b) If you are not employed in a permanent job, a Form I-134 (Affidavit of Support) from a responsible person in the United States or other evidence to show that you are not likely to become a public charge.

4) If your husband or wife is filing an application for permanent residence with yours, he or she also must give INS your marriage certificate and proof for both of you that all prior marriages have been legally ended.

5) If your child is filing an application for permanent residence with yours, he or she also must give INS your marriage certificate and proof that all prior marriages for you and your husband or wife have been

legally ended, unless those documents are being submitted with your husband or wife's application.

C. If you entered the U.S. as a fiancé(e), give INS your marriage certificate. If you are the child of a fiancé(e), give INS your birth certificate and the marriage certificate for your parent's present marriage.

D. If you have resided in the United States continuously since before June 30, 1948, give INS documentary evidence of that fact. Some examples of records that can be used to prove residence are bank, real estate, census, school, insurance, or business records, affidavits of credible witnesses, or any other document that relates to you and shows evidence of your presence in the United States during this period.

E) If you have resided in the United States continuously since before July 1, 1924, INS may be able to create a record of your lawful admission as of the date of your entry. Therefore, if you have resided continuously in the United States since a date before July 1, 1924, it is very important to give evidence establishing that fact.

F. If you are a foreign government official or a representative to an international organization, a member of the family or servant of that person, or a treaty trader or treaty investor or the spouse or child of that person, you must give INS Form I-508. Form I-508 waives all rights, privileges, exemptions, and immunities which you would otherwise have because of that status.

5. How should you prepare this form?

A. Type or print legibly in ink.

B. If you need extra space to complete any item, attach a continuation sheet, indicate the item number, and date and sign each sheet.

C. Answer all questions fully and accurately. If any item does not apply, please write "N/A"

6. Photographs

Give INS two color photographs of yourself taken within 30 days of the date of this application. These photos must have a white background. They must be glossy, un-retouched, and not mounted. The dimension of the facial image must be about 1 inch from the chin to the top of hair; your face should be in ¾ frontal view, showing the right side of the face with the right ear visible. Using pencil or felt pen, lightly print your name on the back of each photograph.

7. Fingerprints

Give INS a completed fingerprint card (Form FD-258) for each applicant between 14 and 70 years of age. Applicants may be fingerprinted by INS employees, other law enforcement officers, outreach centers, charitable and voluntary agencies, or other reputable persons or organizations. The fingerprint card (FD-258), the ink used, and the quality of the prints must meet standards prescribed by the Federal Bureau of Investigation. You must sign the card in the presence of the person taking your fingerprints That person must then sign his or her name and enter the date in the spaces provided. It is important to give all the information called for on the card.

8. Medical examination

You will be required to have a medical examination in conjunction with this application. You may find out more from the INS office that will handle your application.

9. Where must you file?

You must send or take this form and any other required documents to the INS office that has jurisdiction over the place where you live. You will be interviewed. You must bring your temporary entry permit (Form I-94, Arrival Departure Record), and your passport to your interview.

10. What is the fee?

You must pay $50.00 to file this form. **The fee will not be refunded, whether your application is approved or not.** DO NOT MAIL CASH. All checks or money orders, whether U.S. or foreign, must be payable in U.S. currency at a financial institution in the United States. When a check is drawn on the account of a person other than yourself, write your name on the face of the check. If the check is not honored, INS will charge you $5.00.

Pay by check or money order in the exact amount. Make the check or money order payable to "Immigration and Naturalization Service" However,

A. if you live in Guam: Make the check or money order payable to "Treasurer, Guam", or

B. if you live in the U.S. Virgin Islands: Make the check or money order payable to "Commissioner of Finance of the Virgin Islands"

11. What are the penalties for submitting false information?

Title 18, United States Code, Section 1001 states that whoever willfully and knowingly falsifies a material fact, makes a false statement, or makes use of a false document will be fined up to $10,000 or imprisoned up to five years, or both.

12. What is our authority for collecting this information?

We request the information on this form to carry out the immigration laws contained in Title 8, United States Code, Section 1255. We need this information to determine whether a person is eligible for immigration benefits. The information you provide may also be disclosed to other federal, state, local, and foreign law enforcement and regulatory agencies during the course of the investigation required by this Service. You do not have to give this information. However, if you refuse to give some or all of it, your petition may be denied.

It is not possible to cover all the conditions for eligibility or to give instructions for every situation. If you have carefully read all the instructions and still have questions, please contact your nearest INS office.

U.S. Department of Justice
Immigration and Naturalization Service (INS)

Application for Permanent Residence

DO NOT WRITE IN THIS BLOCK

Case ID#	Action Stamp	Fee Stamp
A#		
G-28 or Volag#		
Section of Law ☐ Sec. 209(b), INA ☐ Sec. 214(d), INA ☐ Sec. 13, Act of 9/11/57 ☐ Sec. 245, INA ☐ Sec. 249, INA	Country Chargeable ______	Eligibility Under Sec. 245 ☐ Approved Visa Petition ☐ Dependent of Principal Alien ☐ Special Immigrant ☐ Other ______ Preference ______

A. Reason for this application

I am applying for lawful permanent residence for the following reason: (check the box that applies)

1. ☐ **An immigrant visa number is immediately available to me because**
   - ☐ **A visa petition has already been approved for me** (approval notice is attached)
   - ☐ **A visa petition is being filed with this application**
2. ☐ **I entered as the fiance(e) of a U.S. citizen and married within 90 days** (approval notice and marriage certificate are attached)
3. ☐ **I am an asylee eligible for adjustment**
4. ☐ **Other:** ______

B. Information about you

1. Name (Family name in CAPS) (First) (Middle)

2. Address (Number and Street) (Apartment Number)

(Town or City) (State/Country) (ZIP/Postal Code)

3. Place of Birth (Town or City) (State/Country)

4. Date of Birth (Mo/Day/Yr) **5. Sex** ☐ Male ☐ Female **6. Marital Status** ☐ Married ☐ Single ☐ Widowed ☐ Divorced

7. Social Security Number **8. Alien Registration Number** (if any)

9. Country of Citizenship

10. Have you ever applied for permanent resident status in the U.S.?
☐ Yes ☐ No
(If Yes, give the date and place of filing and final disposition)

11. On what date did you last enter the U.S.?

12. Where did you last enter the U.S.? (City and State)

13. What means of travel did you use? (Plane, car, etc.)

14. Were you inspected by a U.S. immigration officer?
☐ Yes ☐ No

15. In what status did you last enter the U.S.?
(Visitor, student, exchange alien, crewman, temporary worker, without inspection, etc.)

16. Give your name EXACTLY as it appears on your Arrival/Departure Record (Form I-94).

17. Arrival/Departure Record (I-94) Number **18. Visa Number**

19. At what Consulate was your nonimmigrant visa issued? **Date** (Mo/Day/Yr)

20. Have you ever been married before? ☐ Yes ☐ No
If Yes, (Names of prior husbands/wives) (Country of citizenship) (Date marriage ended)

21. Has your husband/wife ever been married before? ☐ Yes ☐ No
If Yes, (Names of prior husbands/wives) (Country of citizenship) (Date marriage ended)

INITIAL RECEIPT	RESUBMITTED	RELOCATED		COMPLETED		
		Rec'd	Sent	Approved	Denied	Returned

FORM I-485 (08-01-85) N

22. List your present husband/wife, all of your sons and daughters, all of your brothers and sisters (If you have none, write "N/A")

Name	Relationship	Place of Birth	Date of Birth	Country of Residence	Applying With You?
					☐ Yes ☐ No
					☐ Yes ☐ No
					☐ Yes ☐ No
					☐ Yes ☐ No
					☐ Yes ☐ No
					☐ Yes ☐ No
					☐ Yes ☐ No
					☐ Yes ☐ No
					☐ Yes ☐ No
					☐ Yes ☐ No

23. List your present and past membership in or affiliation with every organization, association, fund, foundation, party, club, society or similar group in the United States or in any other country or place, and your foreign military service (If this does not apply, write "N/A")

A. ______ 19____ to 19____
B. ______ 19____ to 19____
C. ______ 19____ to 19____
D. ______ 19____ to 19____
E. ______ 19____ to 19____
F. ______ 19____ to 19____
G. ______ 19____ to 19____

24. Have you ever, in or outside the United States:

a) knowingly committed any crime for which you have not been arrested? ☐ Yes ☐ No

b) been arrested, cited, charged, indicted, convicted, fined, or imprisoned for breaking or violating any law or ordinance, including traffic regulations? ☐ Yes ☐ No

c) been the beneficiary of a pardon, amnesty, rehabilitation decree, other act of clemency or similar action? ☐ Yes ☐ No

If you answered Yes to (a), (b), or (c) give the following information about each incident:

	Date	Place (City) (State/Country)	Nature of offense	Outcome of case, if any
1)				
2)				
3)				
4)				
5)				

25. Have you ever received public assistance from any source, including the U.S. Government or any state, county, city or municipality?

☐ Yes ☐ No (If Yes, explain, including the name(s) and Social Security number(s) you used.)

26. Do any of the following relate to you? (Answer Yes or No to each)

A. Have you been treated for a mental disorder, drug addiction, or alcoholism? ☐ Yes ☐ No

B. Have you engaged in, or do you intend to engage in, any commercialized sexual activity? ☐ Yes ☐ No

C. Are you or have you at any time been an anarchist, or a member of or affiliated with any Communist or other totalitarian party, including any subdivision or affiliate? ☐ Yes ☐ No

D. Have you advocated or taught, by personal utterance, by written or printed matter, or through affiliation with an organization:

1) opposition to organized government ☐ Yes ☐ No
2) the overthrow of government by force or violence ☐ Yes ☐ No
3) the assaulting or killing of government officials because of their official character ☐ Yes ☐ No
4) the unlawful destruction of property ☐ Yes ☐ No
5) sabotage ☐ Yes ☐ No
6) the doctrines of world communism, or the establishment of a totalitarian dictatorship in the United States? ☐ Yes ☐ No

E. Have you engaged or do you intend to engage in prejudicial activities or unlawful activities of a subversive nature? ☐ Yes ☐ No

F. During the period beginning March 23, 1933, and ending May 8, 1945, did you order, incite, assist, or otherwise participate in persecuting any person because of race, religion, national origin, or political opinion, under the direction of, or in association with any of the following:

1) the Nazi government in Germany ☐ Yes ☐ No
2) any government in any area occupied by the military forces of the Nazi government in Germany ☐ Yes ☐ No
3) any government established with the assistance or cooperation of the Nazi government of Germany ☐ Yes ☐ No
4) any government that was an ally of the Nazi government of Germany ☐ Yes ☐ No

G. Have you been convicted of a violation of any law or regulation relating to narcotic drugs or marijuana, or have you been an illicit trafficker in narcotic drugs or marijuana? ☐ Yes ☐ No

H. Have you been involved in assisting any other aliens to enter the United States in violation of the law? ☐ Yes ☐ No

I. Have you applied for exemption or discharge from training or service in the Armed Forces of the United States on the ground of alienage and have you been relieved or discharged from that training or service? ☐ Yes ☐ No

J. Are you mentally retarded, insane, or have you suffered one or more attacks of insanity? ☐ Yes ☐ No

K. Are you afflicted with psychopathic personality, sexual deviation, mental defect, narcotic drug addiction, chronic alcoholism, or any dangerous contagious disease? ☐ Yes ☐ No

L. Do you have a physical defect, disease, or disability affecting your ability to earn a living? ☐ Yes ☐ No

M. Are you a pauper, professional beggar, or vagrant? ☐ Yes ☐ No

N. Are you likely to become a public charge? ☐ Yes ☐ No

O. Are you a polygamist or do you advocate polygamy? ☐ Yes ☐ No

P. Have you been excluded from the United States within the past year, or have you at any time been deported from the United States, or have you at any time been removed from the United States at government expense? ☐ Yes ☐ No

Q. Have you procured or have you attempted to procure a visa by fraud or misrepresentation? ☐ Yes ☐ No

R. Are you a former exchange visitor who is subject to, but has not complied with, the two-year foreign residence requirement? ☐ Yes ☐ No

S. Are you a medical graduate coming principally to work as a member of the medical profession, without passing Parts I and II of the National Board of Medical Examiners Examination (or an equivalent examination)? ☐ Yes ☐ No

T. Have you left the United States to avoid military service in time of war or national emergency? ☐ Yes ☐ No

U. Have you committed or have you been convicted of a crime involving moral turpitude? ☐ Yes ☐ No

If you answered Yes to any question above, explain fully (Attach a continuation sheet if necessary):

____

____

____

____

27. ☐ **Completed Form G-325A (Biographic Information) is signed, dated and attached as part of this application.** Print or type so that all copies are legible.

☐ **Completed form G-325A (Biographic Information) is not attached because applicant is under 14 or over 70 years of age.**

Penalties: You may, by law, be fined up to $10,000, imprisoned up to five years, or both, for knowingly and willfully falsifying or concealing a material fact or using any false document in submitting this application.

Your Certification

I certify, under penalty of perjury under the laws of the United States of America, that the above information is true and correct. Furthermore, I authorize the release of any information from my records which the Immigration and Naturalization Service needs to determine eligibility for the benefit that I am seeking.

Signature ____________________ **Date** __________ **Phone Number** __________

Signature of Person Preparing Form if Other than Above

I declare that I prepared this document at the request of the person above and that it is based on all information of which I have any knowledge.

____

(Print Name) (Address) (Signature) (Date)

G-28 ID Number __________

Volag Number __________

Stop Here

*(Applicant is **not** to sign the application below until he or she appears before an officer of the Immigration and Naturalization Service for examination)*

I, ____________________ swear (affirm) that I know the contents of this application that I am signing including the attached documents, that they are true to the best of my knowledge, and that corrections numbered ( ) to ( ) were made by me or at my request, and that I signed this application with my full, true name:

____
(Complete and true signature of applicant)

Signed and sworn to before me by the above-named applicant at ____________________ on ____________________
(Month) (Day) (Year)

____
(Signature and title of officer)

U.S. GOVERNMENT PRINTING OFFICE : 1986 O - 497-584

DEPARTAMENTO DE JUSTICIA
DE LOS ESTADOS UNIDOS
Servicio de Inmigración
y Naturalización

SOLICITUD POR UN EXTRANJERO CON RESIDENCIA LEGAL PERMANENTE PARA OBTENER UNA TARJETA DE REGISTRO DE EXTRANJEROS - TARJETA I–151

INSTRUCCIONES

SIRVASE LEER LAS INSTRUCCIONES CUIDADOSAMENTE. NO SE REEMBOLSARAN LOS DERECHOS.

1. DERECHOS - Si marcó las casillas (a), (b), o (c) del punto 13, deberán pagarse diez dólares (US$10) en concepto de derechos por el registro de esta solicitud. De lo contrario, no se requiere el pago de ningún otro derecho. EL PAGO NO SERA DEVUELTO SEA CUAL FUERE LA RESOLUCION DEL CASO. NO ENVIE DINERO EN EFECTIVO POR CORREO. TODOS LOS PAGOS DEBEN SER ENVIADOS POR LA CANTIDAD EXACTA. El pago por cheque o giro postal debe ser girado contra un banco u otra institución ubicada en los Estados Unidos y ser pagadero en moneda de los Estados Unidos. Si usted es residente de las Islas Vírgenes, el cheque o el giro postal deben hacerse pagaderos al "Commissioner of Finance of the Virgin Islands". Si usted es residente de Guam, el cheque o el giro postal deben hacerse pagaderos al "Treasurer, Guam". Todos los demás solicitantes deben hacer sus cheques o giros postales pagaderos al "Immigration and Naturalization Service". Cuando el cheque se libra contra la cuenta de una persona que no es el solicitante, el nombre del solicitante debe aparecer en el anverso del cheque. Los cheques personales serán aceptados sujeto a las garantías que ofrezcan de cobranza. Un cheque que no se puede cobrar invalidará la solicitud y cualesquiera documentos emitidos en relación con la misma. Si un cheque en pago de derechos no se hace efectivo por el banco contra el que está extendido, se impondrá una costa de cinco dólares (US$5). Si el pago se hace mediante el tipo de giro internacional que no puede enviarse por correo, el giro debe extenderse a la orden del Director de Correos ("Postmaster") de la ciudad en los Estados Unidos a la que se envía la solicitud y en la parte superior de la solicitud se deberá indicar claramente el nombre de esa ciudad, el número del giro y la fecha.

2. DONDE PRESENTAR ESTA SOLICITUD — Si usted está en los Estados Unidos, presente la solicitud a la oficina de Inmigración que tenga jurisdicción en el lugar de su residencia. Si está fuera de los Estados Unidos, presente la solicitud (bien sea personalmente o por conducto de un funcionario consular de los EE.UU.) a la oficina de Inmigración de los EE.UU. que tenga jurisdicción sobre el lugar en que está usted residiendo temporalmente.

3. SANCIONES - LA LEY DISPONE GRAVES SANCIONES PARA LOS QUE A SABIENDAS Y CON INTENCION, FALSIFICAN U OCULTAN UN HECHO IMPORTANTE O USAN UN DOCUMENTO FALSO AL PRESENTAR LA SOLICITUD.

4. ATRIBUCIONES — Título 8 del Código de los Estados Unidos, Secciones 1302 y 1304. Las normas relativas a la divulgación de información para usos de rutina, conforme a la Ley de Protección sobre Información Personal de 1974, están publicadas en el Diario Federal (Federal Register) y se pueden obtener previa solicitud. La información será utilizada por el Servicio para determinar si el solicitante tiene derecho a recibir una tarjeta de registro de extranjero. El no suministrar toda la información solicitada, resultará en la denegación de la solicitud.

DEPARTAMENTO DE JUSTICIA DE LOS ESTADOS UNIDOS
Servicio de Inmigración y Naturalización

Form approved
OMB No. 43–R0040

SOLICITUD POR UN EXTRANJERO CON RESIDENCIA LEGAL PERMANENTE PARA OBTENER UNA TARJETA DE REGISTRO DE EXTRANJEROS

(Tenga la bondad de leer las instrucciones adjuntas)

NOTA: Si usted necesita su tarjeta urgentemente, deberá presentar personalmente esta solicitud y sus correspondientes anexos debidamente llenados en la Oficina del Servicio de Inmigración. Si hace la solicitud en persona, traiga consigo tres fotografías que se ajusten a las especificaciones indicadas en la siguiente hoja de este formulario.

ESCRIBA A MAQUINA O CON UN BOLIGRAFO EN LETRAS DE MOLDE

1. NOMBRE	APELLIDO (Letras mayúsculas) NOMBRE SEGUNDO NOMBRE	TIMBRE
2. DIRECCION POSTAL EN LOS ESTADOS UNIDOS	(NUMERO Y CALLE) (Apt. No.)	
	(CIUDAD) (ESTADO) (NUMERO ZIP)	3. NUMERO DE REGISTRO DE EXTRANJERO

4. NOMBRE QUE USO CUANDO SE INSCRIBIO COMO EXTRANJERO. (SI ES EL MISMO QUE TIENE AHORA, ESCRIBA "SAME".)

5. FECHA DE NACIMIENTO (Mes/día/año)	6. LUGAR DE NACIMIENTO	7. NUMERO DE TELEFONO

8. ADMITIDO A LOS ESTADOS UNIDOS EN: (CIUDAD Y ESTADO)	9. MODO DE TRANSPORTE (Nombre del barco, o línea aérea y número de vuelo, etc.)
10. DESTINO EN LOS EE.UU. CUANDO FUE ADMITIDO	11. CREO QUE MI FICHA SE ENCUENTRA EN LA OFICINA DE INMIGRACION EN (Ciudad y Estado)

12. FECHAS DURANTE LAS QUE PERMANECIO AUSENTE DE LOS EE.UU. POR 1 AÑO O MAS, DESDE QUE FUE ADMITIDO LEGALMENTE COMO RESIDENTE PERMANENTE

13. NECESITO UNA NUEVA TARJETA DEBIDO A QUE:

(A) ☐ Mi documento de registro de extranjero se ha extraviado o ha sido destruído bajo las siguientes circunstancias. (SE REQUIERE EL PAGO EN CONCEPTO DE DERECHOS. VEASE LA INSTRUCCION NUMERO 1) ______

(B) ☐ Mi tarjeta actual está dañada. (Adjunte su antigua tarjeta). (SE REQUIERE EL PAGO EN CONCEPTO DE DERECHOS. VEASE LA INSTRUCCION NUMERO 1)

(C) ☐ Mi nombre ha cambiado. (Adjunte el decreto del tribunal o el certificado de matrimonio y la antigua tarjeta). (SE REQUIERE EL PAGO EN CONCEPTO DE DERECHOS. VEASE LA INSTRUCCION NUMERO 1)

(D) ☐ Debo estar registrado y se me deben tomar las huellas digitales una vez cumplidos los 14 años. (Adjunte su antigua tarjeta). (La Oficina de Inmigración puede tomarle las huellas digitales o usted puede pedir que se las tome un agente en la comisaría de policía o en la oficina de un alguacil. Usted y el agente deben firmar y fechar la tarjeta, una vez que se hayan tomado las huellas digitales. Usted TIENE QUE utilizar la tarjeta para huellas digitales, Formulario FD-258 que nuestra oficina le facilitará). (NO SE REQUIERE PAGO)

(E) ☐ Soy un extranjero que viaja constantemente a los Estados Unidos y se dispone a tomar residencia permanente en los EE. UU. (Adjunte su antigua tarjeta) (NO SE REQUIERE PAGO)

(F) ☐ Recibí una tarjeta incorrecta. (Adjunte su antigua tarjeta) (NO SE REQUIERE PAGO)

(G) ☐ Nunca he recibido una tarjeta. (NO SE REQUIERE PAGO)

(H) ☐ Otra (Explique) (NO SE REQUIERE PAGO) ______

ACTION BLOCK (Para uso del funcionario consular o de inmigración). This applicant was interviewed by me under oath on

______ (Date) at ______ (City).

REMARKS:

______
(Signature and Title)

Serial Number of new I–151, if any ______

☐ GRANTED ☐ DENIED ☐ MAILED ☐ DELIVERED

DATE of ACTION

DD

DISTRICT

______
Signature of Immigration Officer

Fecha y firma del solicitante

______

Fecha y firma de la persona que llena el Formulario en caso de no tratarse del solicitante mismo.

______

☐ Fingerprint card forwarded to the FBI to comply with Section 262 b ______ (Initials and Date)

☐ Call-In Letter Sent ______ (Date)

☐ I-189 to Production Facility ______ (Date)

RECEIVED	TRANS. IN	RET'D. TRANS. OUT	COMPLETED

Form I–90 (Spanish)
(Rev. 5–31–78)N

DEPARTAMENTO DE JUSTICIA DE LOS ESTADOS UNIDOS
Servicio de Inmigración y Naturalización

FECHA:

Número de registro:

Tenga la bondad de presentarse en la oficina que aparece a continuación, a la hora y en el lugar indicados, para mantener una entrevista relativa a su solicitud de la tarjeta de identificación.

Dirección de la oficina	Sala número	Piso número
Fecha y hora	Pregunte por	

INSTRUCCIONES: TRAIGA CONSIGO LO SIGUIENTE:

1. Su tarjeta de registro de extranjero u otro comprobante de registro de extranjero que usted posea actualmente.

2. Fotografias: Tenga la bondad de presentar esta carta al fotógrafo.

   Dos fotografias a color con fondo blanco se requieren. Las fotos deben ser lustrosas, sin ser retocadas, y sencillas (sin ser montadas). La dimensión de la cara debe ser como una pulgada de la barbilla hasta el pico del cabello. La persona debe aparecer en la foto con tres cuartos de la cara en vista con el oído derecho completamente visible.

   Favor de usar lápiz o pluma con punta suave para ligeramente marcar al revés de cada fotografía su nombre completo y el número de su tarjeta de residente permanente de Los Estados Unidos (mica).

   IMPORTANTE: Si las fotografias no cumplen con estos requerimientos, serán regresadas a usted, cual causará demora en procesar su aplicación o petición.

3. Otras: ______

ES IMPORTANTE QUE USTED ACUDA A ESTA CITA Y QUE TRAIGA ESTA CARTA CONSIGO. SI NO LE ES POSIBLE HACERLO, EXPONGA SUS MOTIVOS, FIRME A CONTINUACION Y DEVUELVA ESTA CARTA INMEDIATAMENTE A ESTA OFICINA.

No me es posible acudir a la cita debido a que:	
Firma	Fecha

Form I—90A (Rev. 5—31—78)N

Instructions To Alien Applying for Adjustment of Status

A medical examination is necessary as part of your application for adjustment of status. Please communicate immediately with one of the physicians on the attached list to arrange for your medical examination, which must be completed before your status can be adjusted. The purpose of the medical examination is to determine if you have certain health conditions which may need further follow-up. The information requested is required in order for a proper evaluation to be made of your health status. The results of your examination will be provided to an Immigration officer and may be shared with health departments and other public health or cooperating medical authorities. All expenses in connection with this examination must be paid by you.

The examining physician may refer you to your personal physician or a local public health department and you must comply with some health follow-up or treatment recommendations for certain health conditions before your status will be adjusted.

This form should be presented to the examining physician. You must sign the form in the presence of the examining physician. *The law provides severe penalties for knowingly and willfully falsifying or concealing a material fact or using any false documents in connection with this medical examination. The medical examination must be completed in order for us to process your application.*

Medical Examination and Health Information

A medical examination is necessary as part of your application for adjustment of status. You should go for your medical examination as soon as possible. You will have to choose a doctor from a list you will be given. The list will have the names of doctors or clinics in your area that have been approved by the Immigration and Naturalization Service for this examination. You must pay for the examination. If you become a temporary legal resident and later apply to become a permanent resident, you may need to have another medical examination at that time.

The purpose of the medical examination is to find out if you have certain health conditions which may need further follow-up. The doctor will examine you for certain physical and mental health conditions. You will have to take off your clothes. If you need more tests because of a condition found during your medical examination, the doctor may send you to your own doctor or to the local public health department. For some conditions, before you can become a temporary or permanent resident, you will have to show that you have followed the doctor's advice to get more tests or take treatment.

If you have any records of immunizations (vaccinations), you should bring them to show to the doctor. This is especially important for pre-school and school-age children. The doctor will tell you if any more immunizations are needed, and where you can get them (usually at your local public health department). It is important for your health that you follow the doctor's advice and go to get any immunizations.

One of the conditions you will be tested for is tuberculosis. If you are 15 years of age or older, you will be required to have a chest X-ray examination. ***Exception:*** If you are pregnant or applying for adjustment of status under the Immigration Reform and Control Act of 1986, you may choose to have either a chest X-ray or a tuberculin skin test. If you choose the skin test you will have to return in 2 - 3 days to have it checked. If you do not have any reaction to the skin test you will not need any more tests for tuberculosis. If you do have any reaction to the skin test, you will also need to have a chest X-ray examination. If the doctor thinks you are infected with tuberculosis, you may have to go to the local health department and more tests may have to be done. The doctor will explain these to you.

If you are 14 years of age or younger, you will not need to have a test for tuberculosis unless a member of your immediate family has chest X-ray findings that may be tuberculosis. If you are in this age group and you do have to be tested for tuberculosis, you may choose either the chest X-ray or the skin test.

You must also have a blood test for syphilis if you are 15 years of age or older.

You will also be tested to see if you have the human immunodeficiency virus (HIV) infection. This virus is the cause of AIDS. If you have this virus, it may damage your body's ability to fight off other disease. The blood test you will take will tell if you have been exposed to this virus.

Instructions To Physician Performing the Examination

Please medically examine for adjustment of status the individual presenting this form. The medical examination should be performed according to the U.S. Public Health Service "Guidelines for Medical Examination of Aliens in the United States" and Supplements, which have been provided to you separately.

If the applicant is free of medical defects listed in Section 212(a) of the Immigration and Nationality Act, endorse the form in the space provided. While in your presence, the applicant must also sign the form in the space provided. You should retain one copy for your files and return all other copies in a sealed envelope to the applicant for presentation at the immigration interview.

If the applicant has a health condition which requires follow-up as specified in the "Guidelines for Medical Examination of Aliens in the United States" and Supplements, complete the referral information on the pink copy of the medical examination form, and advise the applicant that appropriate follow-up must be obtained before medical clearance can be granted. Retain the blue copy of the form for your files and return all other copies to the applicant in a sealed envelope. The applicant should return to you when the necessary follow-up has been completed for your final verification and signature. *Do not* sign the form until the applicant has met health follow-up requirements. All medical documents, including chest X-ray films if a chest X-ray examination was performed, should be returned to the applicant upon final medical clearance.

Instructions To Physician Providing Health Follow-up

The individual presenting this form has been found to have a medical condition(s) requiring resolution before medical clearance for adjustment of status can be granted. Please evaluate the applicant for the condition(s) identified.

The requirements for clearance are outlined on the reverse of this page. When the individual has completed clearance requirements, please sign the form in the space provided and return the medical examination form to the applicant.

Medical Clearance Requirements
for Aliens Seeking Adjustment of Status

Medical Condition	Estimated Time For Clearance	Action Required
**Suspected Mental Conditions*	5 - 30 Days	The applicant must provide to a civil surgeon a psychological or psychiatric evaluation from a specialist or medical facility for final classification and clearance.
Tuberculin Skin Test Reaction **and** *Normal Chest X-Ray*	Immediate	The applicant should be encouraged to seek further medical evaluation for possible preventive treatment.
Tuberculin Skin Test Reaction **and** *Abnormal Chest X-Ray* **or** *Abnormal Chest X-Ray* ***(Inactive/Class B)***	10 - 30 Days	The applicant should be referred to a physician or local health department for further evaluation. Medical clearance may not be granted until the applicant returns to the civil surgeon with documentation of medical evaluation for tuberculosis.
Tuberculin Skin Test Reaction **and** *Abnormal Chest X-Ray* **or** *Abnormal Chect X-Ray* ***(Active or Suspected Active/Class A)***	10 - 300 Days	The applicant should obtain an appointment with physician or local health department. If treatment for active disease is started, it must be completed (usually 9 months) before a medical clearance may be granted. At the completion of treatment, the applicant must present to the civil surgeon documentation of completion. If treatment is not started, the applicant must present to the civil surgeon documentation of medical evaluation for tuberculosis.
Hansen's Disease	30 - 210 Days	Obtain an evaluation from a specialist or Hansen's disease clinic. If the disease is indeterminate or Tuberculoid, the applicant must present to the civil surgeon documentation of medical evaluation. If disease is Lepromotous or Borderline (dimorphous) and treatment is started, the applicant must complete at least 6 months and present documentation to the civil surgeon showing adequate supervision, treatment, and clinical response before a medical clearance is granted.
***Venereal Diseases*	1 - 30 Days	Obtain an appointment with a physician or local public health department. An applicant with a reactive serologic test for syphilis must provide to the civil surgeon documentation of evaluation for treatment. If any of the venereal diseases are infectious, the applicant must present to the civil surgeon documentation of completion of treatment.
Immunizations Incomplete	Immediate	Immunizations are not required, but the applicant should be encouraged to go to physician or local health department for appropriate immunizations.
HIV Infection	Immediate	Post-test counseling is not required, but the applicant should be encouraged to seek appropriate post-test counseling.

*** Mental retardation; insanity; previous attack of insanity; psychopathic personality, sexual deviation or mental defect; narcotic drug addition; and chronic alcoholism.**

**** Chancroid; gonorrhea; granuloma inguinale; lymphogranuloma venereum; and syphilis.**

Form I-693 (Rev. 09/01/87) N

U.S. Department of Justice
Immigration and Naturalization Service

OMB #1115-0134
Medical Examination of Aliens Seeking Adjustment of Status

(Please type or print clearly)
I certify that on the date shown I examined:

1. Name (Last in CAPS)

(First) (Middle Initial)

2. Address (Street number and name) (Apt. number)

(City) (State) (ZIP Code)

3. File number (A number)

4. Sex
☐ Male ☐ Female

5. Date of birth (Month/Day/Year)

6. Country of birth

7. Date of examination (Month/Day/Year)

General Physical Examination: I examined specifically for evidence of the conditions listed below. My examination revealed;

☐ No apparent defect, disease, or disability.

☐ The conditions listed below were found (check all boxes that apply).

Class A Conditions

☐ Chancroid
☐ Chronic alcoholism
☐ Gonorrhea
☐ Granuloma inguinale
☐ Hansen's disease, infectious
☐ HIV infection
☐ Insanity
☐ Lymphogranuloma venereum
☐ Mental defect
☐ Mental retardation
☐ Narcotic drug addiction
☐ Previous occurrence of one or more attacks of insanity
☐ Psychopathic personality
☐ Sexual deviation
☐ Syphilis, infectious
☐ Tuberculosis, active

Class B Conditions

☐ Hansen's disease, not infectious ☐ Tuberculosis, not active

☐ Other physical defect, disease or disability (specify below).

Examination for Tuberculosis - Tuberculin Skin Test

☐ Reaction ______ mm ☐ No reaction ☐ Not done

Doctor's name (please print) Date read

Examination for Tuberculosis - Chest X-Ray Report

☐ Abnormal ☐ Normal ☐ Not done

Doctor's name (please print) Date read

Serologic Test for Syphilis

☐ Reactive Titer (confirmatory test performed) ☐ Nonreactive

Test Type

Doctor's name (please print) Date read

Serologic Test for HIV Antibody

☐ Positive (confirmed by Western blot) ☐ Negative

Test Type

Doctor's name (please print) Date read

Immunization Determination (DTP, OPV, MMR, Td-Refer to ***PHS Guidelines*** for recommendations.)

☐ Applicant is current for recommended age-specific immunizations.

☐ Applicant is not current for recommended age-specific immunizations and I have encouraged that appropriate immunizations be obtained.

REMARKS:

Civil Surgeon Referral for Follow-up of Medical Condition

☐ The alien named above has applied for adjustment of status. A medical examination conducted by me identified the conditions above which require resolution before medical clearance is granted or for which the alien may seek medical advice. Please provide follow-up services or refer the alien to an appropriate health care provider. The actions necessary for medical clearance are detailed on the reverse of this form.

Follow-up Information:

The alien named above has complied with the recommended health follow-up.

Doctor's name and address (please type or print clearly) Doctor's signature Date

Applicant Certification:

I certify that I understand the purpose of the medical examination, I authorize the required tests to be completed, and the information on this form refers to me.

Signature Date

Civil Surgeon Certification:

My examination showed the applicant to have met the medical examination and health follow-up requirements for adjustment of status.

Doctor's name and address (please type or print clearly) Doctor's signature Date

The Immigration and Naturalization Service is authorized to collect this information under the provisions of the Immigration and Nationality Act and the Immigration Reform and Control Act of 1986, Public Law 99-603.

I-693

Form I-693 (Rev. 09/01/87) N

ORIGINAL: INS A-FILE

U.S. Department of Justice
Immigration and Naturalization Service (INS)

Petition for Alien Relative

Instructions

Read the instructions carefully. If you do not follow the instructions, we may have to return your petition, which may delay final action.

1. Who can file?

A citizen or lawful permanent resident of the United States can file this form to establish the relationship of certain alien relatives who may wish to immigrate to the United States. You must file a separate form for each eligible relative.

2. For whom can you file?

A. If you are a citizen, you may file this form for:

1) your husband, wife, or unmarried child under 21 years old
2) your unmarried child over 21, or married child of any age
3) your brother or sister if you are at least 21 years old
4) your parent if you are at least 21 years old.

B. If you are a lawful permanent resident you may file this form for:

1) your husband or wife
2) your unmarried child

NOTE: If your relative qualifies under instruction A(2) or A(3) above, separate petitions are not required for his or her husband or wife or unmarried children under 21 years old. If your relative qualifies under instruction B(2) above, separate petitions are not required for his or her unmarried children under 21 years old. These persons will be able to apply for the same type of immigrant visa as your relative.

3. For whom can you *not* file?

You cannot file for people in these four categories:

A. An adoptive parent or adopted child, if the adoption took place after the child became 16 years old, or if the child has not been in the legal custody of the parent(s) for at least two years after the date of the adoption, or has not lived with the parent(s) for at least two years, either before or after the adoption.
B. A stepparent or stepchild, if the marriage that created this relationship took place after the child became 18 years old.
C. A husband or wife, if you were not both physically present at the marriage ceremony, and the marriage was not consummated.
D. A grandparent, grandchild, nephew, niece, uncle, aunt, cousin, or in-law.

4. What documents do you need?

You must give INS certain documents with this form to show you are eligible to file. You must also give INS certain documents to prove the family relationship between you and your relative.

A. For each document needed, give INS the original and one copy. However, because it is against the law to copy a Certificate of Naturalization, a Certificate of Citizenship or an Alien Registration Receipt Card (Form I-151 or I-551), give INS the original only. **Originals will be returned to you.**

B. If you do not wish to give INS the original document, you may give INS a copy. The copy must be certified by:

1) an INS or U.S. consular officer, or
2) an attorney admitted to practice law in the United States, or
3) an INS accredited representative

(INS still may require originals).

C. Documents in a foreign language must be accompanied by a complete English translation. The translator must certify that the translation is accurate and that he or she is competent to translate.

5. What documents do you need to show you are a United States citizen?

A. If you were born in the United States, give INS your birth certificate.
B. If you were naturalized, give INS your original Certificate of Naturalization.
C. If you were born outside the United States, and you are a U.S. citizen through your parents, give INS:
   1) your original Certificate of Citizenship, or
   2) your Form FS-240 (Report of Birth Abroad of a United States Citizen).
D. In place of any of the above, you may give INS your valid unexpired U.S. passport that was initially issued for at least 5 years.
E. If you do not have any of the above and were born in the United States, see the instructions under 8, below, *"What if a document is not available?"*

6. What documents do you need to show you are a permanent resident?

You must give INS your alien registration receipt card (Form I-151 or I-551). Do not give INS a photocopy of the card.

7. What documents do you need to prove family relationship?

You have to prove that there is a family relationship between your relative and yourself.

In any case where a marriage certificate is required, if either the husband or wife was married before, you must give INS documents to show that all previous marriages were legally ended. In cases where the names shown on the supporting documents have changed, give INS legal documents to show how the name change occurred (for example, a marriage certificate, adoption decree, court order, etc.).

Find the paragraph in the following list that applies to the relative you are filing for.

If you are filing for your:

A. **husband or wife,** give INS:

1) your marriage certificate
2) a color photo of you and one of your husband or wife, taken within 30 days of the date of this petition.

Form I-130 (Rev. 06-23-86) Y

I-130

These photos must have a white background. They must be glossy, un-retouched, and not mounted. The dimension of the facial image should be about 1 inch from chin to top of hair in 3/4 frontal view, showing the right side of the face with the right ear visible. Using pencil or felt pen, lightly print name (and Alien Registration Number, if known) on the back of each photograph.

3) a completed and signed Form G-325A (Biographic Information) for you and one for your husband or wife. Except for name and signature, you do not have to repeat on the G-325A the information given on your I-130 petition.

B. **child** and you are the **mother,** give the child's birth certificate showing your name and the name of your child.
C. **child** and you are the **father or stepparent,** give the child's birth certificate showing both parents' names and your marriage certificate.
D. **brother or sister,** give your birth certificate and the birth certificate of your brother or sister showing both parents' names. If you do not have the same mother, you must also give the marriage certificates of your father to both mothers.
E. **mother,** give your birth certificate showing your name and the name of your mother.
F. **father,** give your birth certificate showing the names of both parents and your parents' marriage certificate.
G. **stepparent,** give your birth certificate showing the names of both natural parents and the marriage certificate of your parent to your stepparent.
H. **adoptive parent or adopted child,** give a certified copy of the adoption decree and a statement showing the dates and places you have lived together.

8. What if a document is not available?

If the documents needed above are not available, you can give INS the following instead. (INS may require a statement from the appropriate civil authority certifying that the needed document is not available.)

A. Church record: A certificate under the seal of the church where the baptism, dedication, or comparable rite occurred within two months after birth, showing the date and place of child's birth, date of the religious ceremony, and the names of the child's parents.
B. School record: A letter from the authorities of the school attended (preferably the first school), showing the date of admission to the school, child's date and place of birth, and the names and places of birth of parents, if shown in the school records.
C. Census record: State or federal census record showing the name, place of birth, and date of birth or the age of the person listed.
D. Affidavits: Written statements sworn to or affirmed by two persons who were living at the time and who have personal knowledge of the event you are trying to prove; for example, the date and place of birth, marriage, or death. The persons making the affidavits need not be citizens of the United States. Each affidavit should contain the following information regarding the person making the affidavit: his or her full name, address, date and place of birth, and his or her relationship to you, if any; full information concerning the event; and complete details concerning how the person acquired knowledge of the event.

9. How should you prepare this form?

A. Type or print legibly in ink.
B. If you need extra space to complete any item, attach a continuation sheet, indicate the item number, and date and sign each sheet.
C. Answer all questions fully and accurately. If any item does not apply, please write "N/A".

10. Where should you file this form?

A. If you live in the United States, send or take the form to the INS office that has jurisdiction over where you live.
B. If you live outside the United States, contact the nearest American Consulate to find out where to send or take the completed form.

11. What is the fee?

You must pay $35.00 to file this form. **The fee will not be refunded, whether the petition is approved or not.** DO NOT MAIL CASH. All checks or money orders, whether U.S. or foreign, must be payable in U.S. currency at a financial institution in the United States. When a check is drawn on the account of a person other than yourself, write your name on the face of the check. If the check is not honored, INS will charge you $5.00.

Pay by check or money order in the exact amount. Make the check or money order payable to "Immigration and Naturalization Service". However,

A. if you live in Guam: Make the check or money order payable to "Treasurer, Guam", or
B. if you live in the U.S. Virgin Islands: Make the check or money order payable to "Commissioner of Finance of the Virgin Islands".

12. When will a visa become available?

When a petition is approved for the husband, wife, parent, or unmarried minor child of a United States citizen, these relatives do not have to wait for a visa number, as they are not subject to the immigrant visa limit. However, for a child to qualify for this category, all processing must be completed and the child must enter the United States before his or her 21st birthday.

For all other alien relatives there are only a limited number of immigrant visas each year. The visas are given out in the order in which INS receives properly filed petitions. To be considered properly filed, a petition must be completed accurately and signed, the required documents must be attached, and the fee must be paid.

For a monthly update on dates for which immigrant visas are available, you may call (202) 633-1514

13. What are the penalties for submitting false information?

Title 18, United States Code, Section 1001 states that whoever willfully and knowingly falsifies a material fact, makes a false statement, or makes use of a false document will be fined up to $10,000 or imprisoned up to five years, or both.

14. What is our authority for collecting this information?

We request the information on this form to carry out the immigration laws contained in Title 8, United States Code, Section 1154(a). We need this information to determine whether a person is eligible for immigration benefits. The information you provide may also be disclosed to other federal, state, local, and foreign law enforcement and regulatory agencies during the course of the investigation required by this Service. You do not have to give this information. However, if you refuse to give some or all of it, your petition may be denied.

It is not possible to cover all the conditions for eligibility or to give instructions for every situation. If you have carefully read all the instructions and still have questions, please contact your nearest INS office.

C. (Continued) Information about your alien relative

16. List husband/wife and all children of your relative (if your relative is your husband/wife, list only his or her children)

Name	Relationship	Date of Birth	Country of Birth

17. Address in the United States where your relative intends to reside

(Number and Street) (Town or City) (State)

18. Your relative's address abroad

(Number and Street) (Town or City) (Province) (Country)

19. If your relative's native alphabet is other than Roman letters, write his/her name and address abroad in the native alphabet:

(Name) (Number and Street) (Town or City) (Province) (Country)

20. If filing for your husband/wife, give last address at which you lived together:

(Number and Street)	(Apt. No.)	(Town or City)	(State or Province)	(Country)	From (Month)	(Year)	To (Month)	(Year)

21. Check the appropriate box below and give the information required for the box you checked:

☐ **Your relative will apply for a visa abroad at the American Consulate in** ______________________
(City) (Country)

☐ **Your relative is in the United States and will apply for adjustment of status to that of a lawful permanent resident in the office of the Immigration and Naturalization Service at** ______________________ **. If your relative is not eligible for adjustment of status, he or she**
(City) (State)

will apply for a visa abroad at the American Consulate in ______________________
(City) (Country)

D. Other Information

1. If separate petitions are also being submitted for other relatives, give names of each and relationship.

2. Have you ever filed a petition for this or any other alien before? ☐ **Yes** ☐ **No**

If "Yes" give name, place and date of filing, and result.

Warning: The INS investigates claimed relationships and checks whether documents are real. The INS seeks criminal prosecutions when family relationships are falsified to obtain visas.

Penalties: You may, by law, be fined up to $10,000, imprisoned up to five years, or both, for knowingly and willfully falsifying or concealing a material fact or using any false document in submitting this petition.

Your Certification

I certify, under penalty of perjury under the laws of the United States of America, that the foregoing is true and correct. Furthermore, I authorize the release of any information from my records which the Immigration and Naturalization Service needs to determine eligibility for the benefit that I am seeking.

Signature ______________________ **Date** ____________ **Phone Number** ____________

Signature of Person Preparing Form if Other than Above

I declare that I prepared this document at the request of the person above and that it is based on all information of which I have any knowledge.

(Print Name) (Address) (Signature) (Date)

G-28 ID Number ____________

Volag Number ____________

I-130

U.S. Department of Justice
Immigration and Naturalization Service (INS)

Petition for Alien Relative

OMB No. 1115-0054

DO NOT WRITE IN THIS BLOCK

Case ID#	Action Stamp	Fee Stamp
A#		
G-28 or Volag#		
Section of Law: ☐ 201 (b) spouse ☐ 203 (a)(1) ☐ 201 (b) child ☐ 203 (a)(2) ☐ 201 (b) parent ☐ 203 (a)(4) ☐ 203 (a)(5) AM CON: ______		Petition was filed on ______ (priority date) ☐ Personal Interview ☐ Previously Forwarded ☐ Document Check ☐ Stateside Criteria ☐ Field Investigations ☐ I-485 Simultaneously
REMARKS:		

A. Relationship

1. The alien relative is my:
☐ Husband/Wife ☐ Parent ☐ Brother/Sister ☐ Child

2. Are you related by adoption?
☐ Yes ☐ No

B. Information about you

1. Name (Family name in CAPS) (First) (Middle)

2. Address (Number and Street) (Apartment Number)

(Town or City) (State/Country) (ZIP/Postal Code)

3. Place of Birth (Town or City) (State/Country)

4. Date of Birth (Mo/Day/Yr)

5. Sex ☐ Male ☐ Female

6. Marital Status ☐ Married ☐ Single ☐ Widowed ☐ Divorced

7. Other Names Used (including maiden name)

8. Date and Place of Present Marriage (if married)

9. Social Security Number

10. Alien Registration Number (if any)

11. Names of Prior Husbands/Wives

12. Date(s) Marriage(s) Ended

13. If you are a U.S. citizen, complete the following:
My citizenship was acquired through (check one)

☐ Birth in the U.S.

☐ Naturalization
Give number of certificate, date and place it was issued

☐ Parents
Have you obtained a certificate of citizenship in your own name?
☐ Yes ☐ No
If "Yes", give number of certificate, date and place it was issued

14. If you are a lawful permanent resident alien, complete the following.
Date and place of admission for, or adjustment to, lawful permanent residence:

C. Information about your alien relative

1. Name (Family name in CAPS) (First) (Middle)

2. Address (Number and Street) (Apartment Number)

(Town or City) (State/Country) (ZIP/Postal Code)

3. Place of Birth (Town or City) (State/Country)

4. Date of Birth (Mo/Day/Yr)

5. Sex ☐ Male ☐ Female

6. Marital Status ☐ Married ☐ Single ☐ Widowed ☐ Divorced

7. Other Names Used (including maiden name)

8. Date and Place of Present Marriage (if married)

9. Social Security Number

10. Alien Registration Number (if any)

11. Names of Prior Husbands/Wives

12. Date(s) Marriage(s) Ended

13. Has your relative ever been in the U.S.?
☐ Yes ☐ No

14. If your relative is currently in the U.S., complete the following:
He or she last arrived as a (visitor, student, exchange alien, crewman, stowaway, temporary worker, without inspection, etc.)

Arrival/Departure Record (I-94) Number **Date arrived** (Month/Day/Year)

Date authorized stay expired, or will expire as shown on Form I-94 or I-95

15. Name and address of present employer (if any)

Date this employment began (month/day/year)

I-130

INITIAL RECEIPT	RESUBMITTED	RELOCATED		COMPLETED		
		Rec'd	Sent	Approved	Denied	Returned

Form I-130 (Rev. 06-23-86) Y

U.S. Department of Justice
Immigration and Naturalization Service (INS)

Application by Lawful Permanent Resident for New Alien Registration Receipt Card

Instructions

Read the instructions carefully. If you do not follow the instructions, we may have to return your application, which may delay final action.

1. Who can file?

You may file this form only if

- you are a lawful permanent resident of the United States *and*
- you need a new card.

2. What documents do you need?

A. If you have your old card, you must give it to INS with this application.

B. Give the INS two color photographs of yourself taken within 30 days of the date of this application. These photos must have a white background. They must be glossy, un-retouched, and not mounted. The dimension of the facial image must be about 1 inch from the chin to the top of hair; your face should be in 3/4 frontal view, showing the right side of the face with the right ear visible.

Using pencil or felt pen, lightly print your name (and Alien Registration Number, if you know it) on the back of each photograph.

3. How should you prepare this form?

A. Type or print legibly in ink.

B. If you need extra space to complete any item, attach a continuation sheet, indicate the item number, and date and sign each sheet.

C. Answer all questions fully and accurately. If any item does not apply, please write "N/A."

4. Where should you file this form?

A. If you are in the United States, take this application form **in person** to the INS office having jurisdiction over your place of residence.

B. If you are outside the United States, take this application form **in person** to the United States consulate or INS office that has jurisdiction over the place where you are now living.

5. What is the fee?

If you check (a) or (b) of item 18 "Reason for New Card," you must pay $15.00 to file this form. **The fee will not be refunded, whether the application is approved or not.** DO NOT MAIL CASH. All checks or money orders, whether U.S. or foreign, must be payable in U.S. currency at a financial institution in the United States. When a check is drawn on the account of a person other than yourself, write your name on the face of the check. If the check is not honored, INS will charge you $5.00.

Pay by check or money order in the exact amount. Make the check or money order payable to "Immigration and Naturalization Service." However,

A. if you live in Guam: Make the check or money order payable to "Treasurer, Guam", or

B. if you live in the U.S. Virgin Islands: Make the check or money order payable to "Commission of Finance of the Virgin Islands".

6. What are the penalties for submitting false information?

Title 18, United States Code, Section 1001 states that whoever willfully and knowingly falsifies a material fact, makes a false statement, or makes use of a false document will be fined up to $10,000 or imprisoned up to five years, or both.

7. What is our authority for collecting this information?

We request the information on this form to carry out the immigration laws contained in Title 8, United States Code 1304(c). We need this information to determine whether a person is eligible for immigration benefits. The information you provide may also be disclosed to other federal, state, local, and foreign law enforcement and regulatory agencies during the course of the investigation required by this Service. You do not have to give this information. However, if you refuse to give some or all of it, your application may be denied.

I-90

It is not possible to cover all the conditions for eligibility or to give instructions for every situation. If you have carefully read all the instructions and still have questions, please contact your nearest INS office.

U.S. GOVERNMENT PRINTING OFFICE : 1986 O - 159-542

U.S. Department of Justice
Immigration and Naturalization Service (INS)

Application by Lawful Permanent Resident for New Alien Registration Receipt Card

OMB # 1115-0004

DO NOT WRITE IN THIS BLOCK

Case ID#	Action Stamp	Fee Stamp
A#		
G-28 or Volag#		
F/P to FBI ______ (Date)		Status Verified ☐ CIS ☐ I-151/I-551 ☐ A File ☐ Other ______ Specify
I-89 to TCF ______ (Date)		By ______ Initials on ______ Date Class ______

1. **Name** (Family name in CAPS) (First) (Middle)

2. **Address** (Number and Street) (Apartment Number)

(Town or City) (State/Country) (ZIP/Postal Code)

3. **Place of Birth** (Town or City) (State/Country)

4. **Date of Birth** (Mo/Day/Yr)

5. **Sex** ☐ Male ☐ Female

6. **Name used when admitted as permanent resident** (if different from 1.)

7. **Social Security Number**

8. **Alien Registration Number** (if any)

9. **Country of Citizenship**

10. **Your Mother's First Name**

11. **Your Father's First Name**

12. **The city you lived in when you applied for your immigrant visa or for adjustment to permanent resident status**

13. **Your destination** (city and state) **in the U.S. at the time of your original admission.**

14. **The consulate where your immigrant visa was issued or the INS office where your status was adjusted to permanent resident.**

15. **Your port of admission to the U.S. if you entered with an immigrant visa.**

16. **The date you were admitted or adjusted to permanent resident status.**

17. **List the dates of all your absences from the U.S. lasting one year or longer since you became a permanent resident.**

18. **Reason for new card** (If you check a or b, you must pay $15.00 to file this form.)

a. ☐ My alien registration receipt card was lost, stolen, destroyed, or mutilated. Explain how the card was lost, stolen, destroyed, or mutilated. (Attach the remainder of the card, if it exists.)

b. ☐ My name has been changed. (Attach the decree of the court or the marriage certificate and your old card.)

c. ☐ I am required to be registered and fingerprinted after my 14th birthday. (Attach your old card. You MUST use the fingerprint card Form FD-258, which you can get from any U.S. Consular or INS office.)

d. ☐ I am an alien commuter taking up permanent residence in the U.S. (Attach your old card.)

e. ☐ I received an incorrect card. (Attach your old card and explain what is wrong with it.)

f. ☐ I never received my card.

g. ☐ Other (Explain) ______

Penalties: You may, by law, be fined up to $10,000 or imprisoned up to five years, or both, for knowingly and willfully falsifying or concealing a material fact or using any false document in submitting this application.

Your Certification

I certify, under penalty of perjury under the laws of the United States of America, that the above information is true and correct. Furthermore, I authorize the release of any information from my records which the Immigration and Naturalization Service needs to determine if I am eligible for the benefit that I am seeking.

Signature ______ **Date** ______ **Phone Number** ______

Signature of Person Preparing Form if Other than Above

I declare that I prepared this document at the request of the person above and that it is based on all information of which I have any knowledge.

(Print Name) (Address) (Signature) (Date)

G-28 ID Number ______

Volag Number ______

INITIAL RECEIPT	RESUBMITTED	RELOCATED		COMPLETED		
		Rec'd	Sent	Approved	Denied	Returned

FORM I-90 (Rev. 06-23-86) Y

UNITED STATES DEPARTMENT OF JUSTICE
IMMIGRATION AND NATURALIZATION SERVICE

APPLICATION TO FILE PETITION FOR NATURALIZATION

INSTRUCTIONS TO THE APPLICANT

(Tear off this instruction sheet before filling out this form)

You must be at least 18 years old to file a petition for naturalization. Using ink or a typewriter, answer every question in the application form, whether you are male or female. If you need more space for an answer, write "Continued" in your answer, then finish your answer on a sheet of paper this size, giving the number of the question.

YOU WILL BE EXAMINED UNDER OATH ON THE ANSWERS IN THIS APPLICATION WHEN YOU APPEAR FOR YOUR NATURALIZATION EXAMINATION.

If you wish to be called for examination at the same time as a relative who is applying for naturalization is called, attach a separate sheet so stating, and show the name and the Alien Registration Number of that relative.

1. **YOU MUST SEND WITH THIS APPLICATION THE FOLLOWING ITEMS (1), (2), (3) AND (4):**

(1) **Photographs of your Face:**

a. Three identical unglazed copies, size 2 x 2 inches only.

b. Taken within the last 30 days.

c. Distance from top of head to point of chin to be 1¼ inches.

d. On thin paper, with light background, showing front view without hat.

e. In natural color or black and white, and not machine-made.

f. Unsigned (but write Alien Registration Number lightly in pencil in center of reverse side).

(2) **Fingerprint Chart**—Complete the personal data items such as name, aliases, weight, date of birth, etc. Write in your Alien Registration Number in the space marked "Miscellaneous No. MNO" or "Your No. OCA" and take the chart with these instructions to any police station, sheriff's office, or office of the Immigration and Naturalization Service for fingerprinting. You must then sign the chart in the presence of the officer taking the fingerprints and have him/her sign his/her name and title and fill in the date in the spaces provided. DO NOT BEND, FOLD OR CREASE THE FINGERPRINT CHART.

(3) **Biographic Information.**—Complete every item in the Biographic Information form furnished you with this application and sign your name on the line provided. If you have ever served in the Armed Forces of the United States, obtain and complete also an extra yellow sheet of the form, bearing the number G-325B.

(4) **U.S. Military Service.**—If your application is based on your military service, obtain and complete Form N—426, "Request for Certification of Military or Naval Service."

2. **FEE.**—DO NOT SEND any fee with this application unless you are also applying for a certificate of citizenship for a child (see Instruction 6).

3. **ALIEN REGISTRATION RECEIPT CARD.**—DO NOT SEND your Alien Registration Receipt Card with this application.

4. **EXAMINATION ON GOVERNMENT AND LITERACY.**—Every person applying for naturalization must show that he or she has a knowledge and understanding of the history, principles, and form of government of the United States. THERE IS NO EXEMPTION FROM THIS REQUIREMENT, and you will therefore be examined on these subjects when you appear before the examiner with your witnesses.

You will also be examined on your ability to read, write and speak English. If on the date of your examination you are more than 50 years of age and have been a lawful permanent resident of the United States for 20 or more years, you will be exempt from the English language requirements of the law. If you are exempt, you may take the examination in any language you wish.

5. **OATH OF ALLEGIANCE.**—You will be required to take the following oath of allegiance to the United States in order to become a citizen:

DEPARTAMENTO DE JUSTICIA DE LOS ESTADOS UNIDOS
SERVICIO DE INMIGRACION Y NATURALIZACION

SOLICITUD PARA PRESENTAR LA PETICION DE NATURALIZACION
INSTRUCCIONES AL SOLICITANTE

(Separe esta hoja de instrucciones antes de radicar este formulario.)

Usted debe tener por lo menos 18 años de edad para poder presentar una petición de naturalización. Empleando tinta o una máquina de escribir, conteste cada pregunta en el formulario de solicitud, ya sea usted hombre o mujer. Si usted necesita más espacio para contestar una pregunta, escriba "Continúa" en su respuesta y luego termine su contestación en una hoja de papel de este tamaño, indicando el número de la pregunta.

CUANDO USTED COMPAREZCA PARA SU PRUEBA DE NATURALIZACION, SERA INTERROGADO BAJO JURAMENTO SOBRE LAS RESPUESTAS DADAS EN ESTA SOLICITUD.

Si usted desea ser llamado para la prueba al mismo tiempo que es llamado un familiar suyo que ha solicitado la naturalización, prenda otra hoja declarándolo así, e indique el nombre y el Número de Inscripición como Extranjero de ese familiar.

1. JUNTAMENTE CON ESTA SOLICITUD, USTED TIENE QUE ENVIAR TAMBIEN LOS SIGUIENTES PARTICULARES (1), (2), (3) y (4):

(1) *Fotografías de su Rostro:*
- a. Tres copias idénticas, sin satinar, tamaño 2 × 2 solamente.
- b. Tomadas durante los últimos 30 días.
- c. La distancia desde la coronilla de la cabeza hasta la punta de la barbilla debe ser 1¼ pulgadas.
- d. En papel diáfano, con un fondo claro, mostrando la cara, sin sombrero.
- e. En color natural, o blanco y negro, y que no hayan sido hechas a máquina.
- f. No las firme (pero escriba suavemente con lápiz, en el centro del reverso, su Número de Inscripción como Extranjero).

(2) *Tarjeta de Huellas Digitales*—Complete los datos de información personal, tales como nombre, alias, peso, fecha de nacimiento, etc. Escriba su Número de Inscripción como Extranjero en el espacio marcado "Miscellaneous No. MNO" o "Your No. OCA" y lleve la tarjeta con estas instrucciones a cualquier cuartel de policía, oficina de alguacil u oficina del Servicio de Inmigración y Naturalización para que allí le tomen las huellas digitales. Usted deberá entonces firmar dicha tarjeta en presencia del funcionario que le ha tomado las huellas digitales y cerciorarse de que él (o ella) firme su nombre y cargo, y la fecha, en los espacios en blanco que aparecen para ello. NO DOBLE, ARRUGUE O PLIEGUE LA TARJETA DE HUELLAS DIGITALES.

(3) *Información Biográfica.*—Complete cada detalle o particular en el formulario de Información Biográfica que se le suministra a usted con esta solicitud, y firme su nombre en la línea que aparece para ello. Si usted alguna vez ha prestado servicios en las Fuerzas Armadas de Estados Unidos, obtenga y complete también una hoja amarilla adicional del formulario, que lleva el número G-325B.

(4) *Servicio Militar en Estados Unidos.*—Si su solicitud se basa en su servicio militar, obtenga y complete el Formulario N-426, "Petición Para la Certificación de Servicio Militar o Naval".

2. **HONORARIOS.**—NO ENVIE honorario alguno con esta solicitud, excepto que también esté usted solicitando un certificado de ciudadanía para un hijo (Véase Instrucción 6).

3. **COMPROBANTE DE INSCRIPCION COMO EXTRANJERO.**—NO ENVIE su Comprobante de Inscripción Como Extranjero (Alien Registration Receipt Card) con esta solicitud.

4. **PRUEBA DE ALFABETISMO Y SISTEMA DE GOBIERNO.**—Toda persona que solicite la naturalización tiene que demostrar tener conocimiento y entender la historia, los principios y el sistema de gobierno de los Estados Unidos. NADIE ESTA EXENTO DE ESTE REQUISITO y, por lo tanto, se someterán a prueba sus conocimientos sobre estas materias cuando usted comparezca ante el Examinador.

También se someterá a prueba su habilidad para leer, escribir y hablar inglés. Si en la fechá de su prueba usted tiene más de 50 años de edad o ha estado residiendo legalmente como residente permanente en los Estados Unidos durante 20 años o más, usted estará exento de los requisitos que dispone la ley sobre el conocimiento del idioma inglés. Si llena esos requisitos para quedar exento, entonces puede tomar la prueba en cualquier idioma que usted así lo desee.

5. **JURAMENTO DE FIDELIDAD.**—Para poder convertirse en ciudadano, usted deberá prestar el siguiente juramento de fidelidad a los Estados Unidos:

I hereby declare, on oath, that I absolutely and entirely renounce and abjure all allegiance and fidelity to any foreign prince, potentate, state or sovereignty, of whom or which I have heretofore been a subject or citizen; that I will support and defend the Constitution and laws of the United States of America against all enemies, foreign and domestic; that I will bear true faith and allegiance to the same; that I will bear arms on behalf of the United States when required by the law; that I will perform noncombatant service in the armed forces of the United States when required by the law; that I will perform work of national importance under civilian direction when required by the law; and that I take this obligation freely without any mental reservation or purpose of evasion; so help me God.

If you cannot promise to bear arms or perform noncombatant service because of religious training and belief, you may omit those promises when taking the oath.

"Religious training and belief" means a person's belief in a relation to a Supreme Being involving duties superior to those arising from any human relation, but does not include essentially political, sociological, or philosophical views or a merely personal moral code.

6. **THIS BLOCK APPLIES ONLY TO APPLICANTS WHO HAVE FOREIGN-BORN CHILDREN WHO ARE UNDER 18 YEARS OF AGE.**

Some or all of your *own* foreign-born children (Not Step-Children) who are not yet citizens may possibly become United States citizens automatically when you are naturalized. This will happen:

(1) If the child is a lawful permanent resident of the United States and still under 18 years of age when you are naturalized, and

(2) The child's other parent is already a citizen or becomes a citizen before or at the same time that you become naturalized. If, however, the child's other parent is deceased, or if you are divorced and have custody of the child, then it makes no difference that the child's other parent was or is an alien.

(3) If your child is illegitimate and you are the mother, only (1) above applies.

(4) If the child is adopted, and was adopted before its 16th birthday and is in your custody.

If you wish, you can apply for a Certificate of Citizenship for any of these children, which will show that they are United States citizens. If you do not want such a Certificate, write "DO NOT" in Question (34), page 3; if you do want such a Certificate, write "DO" in Question (34), page 3, and send the following with this application:

(1) **Fee.** Fifteen dollars ($15) for each child for whom a certificate is desired. DO NOT SEND CASH IN THE MAIL. ALL FEES MUST BE SUBMITTED IN THE EXACT AMOUNT. If you mail your application, attach a money order or check, payable to *Immigration and Naturalization Service, Department of Justice.* (Exceptions: If you reside in the Virgin Islands, remittance must be payable to Commissioner of Finance, Virgin Islands; and if in Guam, to Treasurer, Guam). Personal checks are accepted subject to collectibility. An uncollectible check will render the application and any documents issued pursuant thereto invalid. A charge of $5.00 will be imposed if a check in payment of a fee is not honored by the bank on which it is drawn. The fee will be refunded if for any reason you are not naturalized in time or the child does not qualify for the certificate.

(2) **Personal Description Form.**—A completed Form N—604 for each child.

(3) **Documents.**—The documents applicable to your case listed in the blocks below. If you want any of the original documents returned to you, and if the law does not prohibit the making of copies, a photocopy of the document should be sent with the original document.

Any document in a foreign language must be accompanied by a summary translation in English. A summary translation is a condensation or abstract of the document's text. The translator must certify that he is competent to translate and that the translation is accurate.

(4) **Photographs.**—Follow Instruction No. 1 (1) and send three (3) photographs of each child. Write the child's Alien Registration Number on the back of the photographs, lightly in pencil.

DOCUMENTS REQUIRED WITH THIS APPLICATION

1. **Child's birth certificate.**
2. **Your marriage certificate to child's other parent.**
3. **If you or the other parent were married before the marriage to each other, death certificate or divorce decree showing the termination of any previous marriage of each parent.**
4. **If the other parent became a citizen at birth, birth certificate of other parent.**
5. **If the child's other parent is deceased, or if you are divorced from the child's other parent, the death certificate or the divorce decree.**
6. **If the child is adopted, adoption decree.**

SECONDARY EVIDENCE

If it is not possible to obtain any one of the required documents shown in the block above, consideration may be given to the following documents. In such case you must present a written explanation as to why the document listed in the block above is not being presented, together with a statement from the official custodian of the record showing that the document is not available.

1. ***Baptismal certificate.*—A certificate under the seal of the church where the baptism occurred, showing date and place of child's birth, date of baptism, the names of the child's parents, and names of the godparents, if shown.**
2. ***School record.*—A letter from the school authorities having jurisdiction over the school attended (preferably the first school), showing date of admission to the school, child's date of birth or age at that time, place of birth, and the names and places of birth of parents, if shown in the school records.**
3. **If you or the other parent were married before the marriage tc each other, death certificate or divorce decree showing the termination of any person(s) listed.**
4. ***Affidavits.*—Notarized affidavits of two persons who were living at the time, and who have personal knowledge of the event you are trying to prove—for example, the date and place of a birth, marriage, or death. The persons making the affidavits may be relatives and need not be citizens of the United States. Each affidavit should contain the following information regarding the person making the affidavit; His (Her) full name and address; date and place of birth; relationship to you, if any; full information concerning the event; and complete details concerning how he (she) acquired knowledge of the event.**

Declaro por la presente, bajo juramento, que renuncio y abjuro, en forma total y absoluta, a toda obediencia o fidelidad a cualquier príncipe, potentado, soberano o Estado extranjero de quien o del cual en tiempos pasados fui súbdito o ciudadano; que apoyaré y defenderé la Constitución y las leyes de los Estados Unidos contra cualquier enemigo, interno o externo; que tendré fe verdadera en y seré leal a los Estados Unidos; que tomaré las armas en favor de Estados Unidos cuando la ley así lo requiera; que prestaré servicios como no combatiente en las fuerzas armadas de Estados Unidos cuando la ley así lo requiera; que desempeñaré labores de importancia nacional bajo una dirección civil cuando la ley así lo requiera; y que asumo esta obligación libremente, sin ninguna reserva mental, ni con fines evasivos; así sea, quiéralo Dios.

Si usted no puede prometer tomar las armas o prestar servicios como no combatiente debido a sus creencias e instrucción religiosa, entonces usted puede omitir estas dos promesas cuando preste el juramento.

"Creencia e instrucción religiosa" significa la creencia de la persona en un Ser Supremo, que implican deberes superiores a aquellos que surgen de cualquier relación humana, pero que no incluyen, substancialmente, puntos de vista políticos, sociológicos o filosóficos, o meramente un código de ética personal.

6. **ESTA PARTE SE APLICA SOLAMENTE A LOS SOLICITANTES QUE TIENEN HIJOS MENORES DE 18 AÑOS DE EDAD, NACIDOS EN EL EXTRANJERO.**

Al usted naturalizarse, algunos de sus propios hijos nacidos en el extranjero, o todos (no los hijastros), que todavía no son ciudadanos, posiblemente podrían convertirse automáticamente en ciudadanos de Estados Unidos. Esto sucedería:

(1) Si el niño es un residente legal permanente en Estados Unidos y todavía es menor de 18 años de edad al usted naturalizarse, y

(2) Si el otro padre del niño ya es ciudadano, o se convertirá en ciudadano antes o al mismo tiempo en que usted adquiera la naturalización. Sin embargo, si el otro padre del niño ha fallecido, o si usted se ha divorciado y tiene la potestad del niño, entonces no importa que el otro padre del niño sea o fuere extranjero.

(3) Si su niño no es hijo de matrimonio y usted es la madre, entonces sólo la sección (1) arriba enumerada es aplicable.

(4) Si el niño es un hijo adoptivo, y fue adoptado antes de que cumpliera los 16 años de edad, y está al abrigo de usted.

Si usted así lo desea, puede solicitar un Certificado de Ciudadanía para cualquiera de estos niños, lo que será prueba de que ellos son ciudadanos de Estados Unidos. Si usted **no desea** este Certificado, escriba "DO NOT" en la Pregunta (34), página 3; por el contrario, si usted **desea** este Certificado, escriba "DO" en la Pregunta (34), página 3, y envíe **lo siguiente** con esta solicitud:

(1) *Honorarios*. Quince dólares ($15) por cada niño para quien usted desea un certificado. NO ENVIE DINERO EN EFECTIVO POR CORREO. TODOS LOS HONORARIOS TIENEN QUE SER SOMETIDOS EN SU TOTALIDAD. Si usted envía su solicitud por correo, remita adjunto un cheque o giro postal, pagadero al Servicio de Inmigración y Naturalización, Departamento de Justicia. (Excepciones: Si usted reside en Islas Vírgenes, la letra de cambio debe ser hecha pagadera al Comisionado de Finanzas, Islas Vírgenes; y si usted reside en Guam, al Tesorero de Guam.) La aceptación de los cheques personales está sujeta a que sean cobrables. Un cheque que no sea cobrable invalidará la solicitud y cualquier otro documento emitido con esa condición. Se impondrá un recargo de $5.00 si el cheque en pago de los honorarios no es aceptado por el banco donde se ha girado. Los honorarios le serán devueltos si por alguna razón usted no se naturaliza, o si el niño no califica para el certificado.

(2) *Formulario de Descripción Personal*.—Por cada niño, debe completarse un Formulario N-604.

(3) *Documentos*.—Los documentos aplicables a su caso, son enumerados más adelante. Si desea que cualquiera de los documentos originales le sea devuelto, y si la ley no prohibe que se saquen copias, una fotocopia del documento, y el original, deben ser les enviados a usted.

Cualquier documento en un idioma extranjero tiene que ser acompañado por un resumen en idioma inglés. Dicho resumen en inglés será un sumario o epítome del documento. El traductor debe certificar que es competente para hacer la traducción y que la traducción es fiel y exacta.

(4) *Fotografías*.—Siga la Instrucción No. 1 (1) y envíe tres (3) fotografías de cada niño. Escriba suavemente con lápiz, en el reverso de las fotografías, el Número de Inscripción como Extranjero del niño.

DOCUMENTOS QUE SE REQUIEREN CON ESTA SOLICITUD

1. El certificado de nacimiento del niño.
2. Su certificado de matrimonio con el otro padre del niño.
3. Si usted o el otro padre habían contraído matrimonio anteriormente, antes de casarse uno con el otro, el certificado de defunción o divorcio, demostrando, cada padre, la terminación del matrimonio anterior.
4. Si el otro padre se convirtió en ciudadano al nacer, el certificado de nacimiento del otro padre.
5. Si el otro padre del niño ha fallecido, o si usted se ha divorciado del otro padre del niño, el certificado de defunción, o el certificado de divorcio.
6. Si el niño ha sido adoptado, el decreto de adopción.

EVIDENCIA SECUNDARIA

Si no es posible conseguir ninguno de los documentos requeridos que son enumerados en la parte superior, se podrían considerar los documentos que vamos a enumerar a continuación. En este caso, usted tendrá que presentar una explicación por escrito, informando la razón por la que no ha sido posible someter los documentos enumerados en la parte de arriba, juntamente con una declaración del custodio oficial de los archivos atestiguando que dichos documentos no están disponibles.

1. *Certificado de Bautismo*.—Un certificado autenticado por el sello de la iglesia donde se efectuó el bautismo, indicando la fecha y el lugar del nacimiento del niño, los nombres de los padres del niño, y los nombres de los padrinos, si figuran en el acta.

2. *Expediente Escolar*.—Una carta de las autoridades escolares con jurisdicción sobre la escuela (preferiblemente la primera escuela), señalando la fecha de ingreso del niño a la escuela, la fecha de nacimiento del niño o su edad en esa época, lugar donde nació el niño, y los nombres y lugares donde nacieron sus padres, de figurar este último dato en las actas de la escuela.
3. Si usted o el otro padre habían contraído matrimonio anteriormente, antes de casarse uno con el otro, el certificado de defunción o de divorcio, demontrando la terminación del vínculo civil con cualquier otra persona indicada.
4. *Declaración Jurada*.—Declaraciones Juradas ante un Notario de dos personas que vivían en esa época y que tienen conocimiento personal del hecho que usted está tratando de probar o autenticar—por ejemplo, la fecha y el lugar de un nacimiento, matrimonio o fallecimiento. Las personas que presten estas declaraciones pueden ser familiares suyos y no tienen que ser ciudadanos de los Estados Unidos. Cada declaración jurada ante Notario debe contener la siguiente información con respecto a la persona que esta haciendo la declaración: nombre y dirección (completos); fecha y lugar de nacimiento; su vínculo con usted, si hay alguno; completa información sobre el hecho; y plenos detalles con respecto a cómo él (o ella) adquirieron conocimiento del hecho.

Iglesias y Grupos de la Comunidad Designados

Courtesy of the Outreach Program—U. S. Immigration and Naturalization Service.

ALABAMA

Catholic Social Services
211 South Catherine Street, #2
Mobile, AL 36604
(205) 471–1305

ARKANSAS

Catholic Charities
2500 North Tyler Street
Little Rock, AR 72207
(501) 664–0340

ARIZONA

Portable Practical Educational Preparation, Inc.
1107 G. Avenue
Douglas, AZ 85607
(602) 364–4405

Lutheran Social Ministry
14010 North El Mirage Road
El Mirage, AZ 85335
(602) 937–0500

Central American Refugee Project
1407 North 2nd Street
Phoenix, AZ 85004
(602) 253–3657

Catholic Social Services of Phoenix
1825 West Northern Avenue
Phoenix, AZ 85021
(602) 997–6105

Catholic Social Services
21 East Speedway
P.O. Box 5746
Tucson, AZ
(602) 623–0344

SER-JOBS for Progress
205 Main Street
P.O. Box 352
Yuma, AZ 85364
(602) 783–4414

CALIFORNIA

World Relief
Primera Iglesia Bautista
2657 Niles
Bakersfield, CA 93306
(805) 324–4020

Metropolitan Immigration Centers of America

1919 Manolia Boulevard
Burbank, CA 91506
(818) 841–1090

International Assistance
21054 Sherman Way, Suite 265
Canoga Park, CA 91303
(818) 716–0188

International Assistance
4065 East Whittier Boulevard, Suite 204
East Los Angeles, CA 90023
(213) 264–7001

Immigrant Legal Resource Center
1359 Bay Road
East Palo Alto, CA 94303
(415) 853–1600

U. S. Consultation Services
2112 Highway 86, Suites 4 & 5
El Centro, CA 92243
(619) 353–3941

Asistencia Inmigracion del Condado Norte
935 Mission Avenue
Escondido, CA 92025
(619) 489–8172

World Relief
First Hispanic Church
1304 Mariposa Street
Fresno, CA 93706
(209) 268–4833

International Assistance
Imperial Savings Building
2650 Zoe Avenue, 3rd Floor
Huntington Park, CA 90255
(215) 585–0764

Los Angeles County Bar Association
Immigration Legal Assistance Project
300 North Los Angeles Street, Room 4349
Los Angeles, CA 90012
(213) 485–1872

Immigration Amnesty Service, Inc.
132 West First Street, #224
Los Angeles, CA 90012
(213) 613–1250
(213) 613–1295

Catholic Charities
Archdiocese of Los Angeles
1400 9th Street
Los Angeles, CA 90015-0095
(213) 251–3465
(213) 620–8507

Catholic Charities Center
535 Cooper Road
Oxnard, CA 93030
(805) 487–5567

Alien Legalization for Agriculture (ALFA)
1601 Exposition Boulevard, FB-8
Sacramento, CA 95815-5195
(916) 924–4019

Catholic Social Services
1705 2nd Avenue
Salinas, CA 93905
(408) 422–0602

Catholic Community Services
Refugee and Immigration Office
4643 Mission Gorge Place
San Diego, CA 92120
(619) 287–9454

Immigration Services of Santa Rosa
P.O. Box 4377
606 Chatsworth Drive
San Fernando, CA 91340
(818) 361–4341

World Relief
First Spanish Baptist Church
976 South Van Ness
San Francisco, CA 94110
(415) 647–1001

Your Ag Employers Care
1621 East 17th Street, Suite S
Santa Ana, CA 92701
(714) 550–0660

Metropolitan Immigration Centers of America
6523 Hazeltine Avenue
Van Nuys, CA 91401
(801) 902–9713
(801) 988–8672

COLORADO

Catholic Community Services
8715 East Pikes Peak
Colorado Springs, CO 80909
(303) 636–1537

Justice Information Center
1129 Cherokee Street
Denver, CO 80204
(303) 623–5750

Lutheran Social Service of Colorado
Legalization Program
3245 West 31st Avenue
Denver, CO 80211
(303) 458–0222

Catholic Immigration Service
Diocese of Pueblo
119 West 6th Street
Pueblo, CO 81003
(303) 543–7837

CONNECTICUT

Catholic Charities
Migration and Refugee Services
125 Market Street
Hartford, CT 06103
(203) 548–0059

DISTRICT OF COLUMBIA

Legalization Assistance Center for Undocumented Aliens
1118 22nd Street, NW, Suite 300
Washington, DC 20037
(202) 223–0283
(202) 223–1811

Travelers Aid Society of Washington, DC
1015 12th Street, NW
Washington, DC 20005
(202) 347–0101

Congress of Racial Equality
National Press Building
529 14th Street, NW, Suite 11020
Washington, DC 20036
(202) 737–5030

DELAWARE

Service for Foreign Born
Dover Air Force Base
Personnel Building, Room 120
Dover, DE 19901
(302) 678–6389
(302) 678–7011

FLORIDA

Martin Luther King, Jr.
Farm Workers Fund
1000 C West Main Street
Avon Park, FL 33825
(813) 452–0170

Lutheran Ministries of Florida
Legalization Services
3565 Davie Boulevard
Fort Lauderdale, FL 33312
(305) 792–6618

Florida Fruit & Vegetable Association
12175 N.W. 98th Street
P.O. Box 5245
Hialeah, FL 33113
(305) 823–1146

Travelers Aid Society of Jacksonville
271 West Church Street
Jacksonville, FL 32202
(904) 356–0249

Private Immigration Agency
7880-B Biscayne Boulevard
Miami, FL 33138
(305) 751–8212/8217;
(305) 854–4950

World Relief
701 S.W. 27th Avenue, Suite 710
Miami, FL 33135
(305) 541–8320

Catholic Social Services, Inc.
1771 North Semoran Boulevard
Orlando, FL 32807
(305) 658–0110

Lutheran Immigration and Refugee Services
Beth-El Mission
14th Street and Shell Point Road
P.O. Box 1706
Ruskin, FL 33570
(813) 645–1254

GEORGIA

Latin American Association, Inc.
2581 Piedmont Road N.E., Suite 111
Atlanta, GA 30324
(404) 231–0940

Catholic Diocese of Savannah
Office of Social Ministry
St. John's Center
Grimball Point Road
Savannah, Ga 31406
(912) 238–2351

HAWAII

Catholic Immigration Center
712 North School Street
Honolulu, HI 96817
(808) 528–5233

Kahili Palama Immigrant Service Center
720 North King Street
Honolulu, HI 96817
(808) 845–3918

IDAHO

Ecumenical Ministries
4900 North Five-Mile Road
Boise, ID 83704
(208) 376–4529

Catholic Social Services
St. Therese's Church Hall
125 West 16th Street
P.O. Box 1223
Burley, ID 83318
(208) 678–5453

Idaho Falls Regional Information and Referral Service
AYUDA Network
545 Shoup Street, Room 233

P.O. Box 2246
Idaho Falls, ID 83402–2246
(208) 524–2433

ILLINOIS

Catholic Family Center
315 North Root Street
Aurora, IL 60505
(312) 851–1890

The Salvation Army
5040 North Pulaski Road
Chicago, IL 60630
(312) 725–1100

Private Immigration Agency
4142 West 26th Street
Chicago, IL 60623
(312) 277–4142

World Relief
3507 West Lawrence, Suite 206
Chicago, IL 60608
(312) 583–9191

Catholic Archdiocese of Chicago
Legalization Outreach Services
2380 South Halsted Street
Chicago, IL 60608
(312) 263–4299 (HOTLINE)
(312) 263–4298 (ENG)
(312) 263–4299 (SPAN)
(312) 263–4665 (POLI)

Travelers and Immigrants Aid of Chicago
4750 North Sheridan Avenue, Suite 200
Chicago, IL 60640
(312) 489–7303

Episcopal Legalization Center
Chaplaincy Use Book Store
808 Glenflora Avenue
Waukegan, IL 60085
(312) 244–7676

INDIANA

Catholic Charities
Diocese of Gary
973 West 6th Avenue
Gary, IN 46402
(219) 882–2720

Legal Services Organization of Indiana
107 North Pennsylvania Street, Suite 1008
Indianapolis, IN 46204
(317) 631–1395

IOWA

Catholic Diocese of Davenport
Immigration Counseling and Resettlement Office
2706 Gaines Street
Davenport, IA 52804
(319) 324–1911

Proteus Employment Opportunities
1406 Nebraska Street
Sioux City, IA 51105
(712) 258–0094

KANSAS

Harvest America Corporation
118 Grant Avenue
Garden Avenue, KS 67846
(316) 275–1619

Catholic Archdiocese of Kansas City
Legalization Office (El Centro, Inc.)
736 Shawnee Avenue

Kansas City, KS 66105
(913) 621–4500

El Centro de Servicios Para Hispanos
1109 Seward
Topeka, KS 66616
(913) 232–8207

Catholic Social Services
Office of Hispanic Affairs
940 South St. Francis
Wichita, KS 67211
(316) 269–4587

KENTUCKY

Catholic Charities of Louisville
2911 South 4th Street
Louisville, KY 40208
(502) 636–9263

LOUISIANA

Catholic Community Services
1800 South Arcadian Thruway
P.O. Box 65688
Baton Rouge, LA 70896
(504) 346–0660

Catholic Social Services
Migration and Refugee Services
1408 Carmel Avenue
Lafayette, LA 70501
(318) 261–5535

Travelers Aid Society of Greater New Orleans
936 St. Charles Avenue, Suite 200
New Orleans, LA 70130
(504) 525–8726

MAINE

Catholic Charities
107 Elm Street
Portland, ME 04101
(207) 871–7437

MARYLAND

Catholic Archdiocese of Baltimore Hispanic Center
10 South Wolfe Street
Baltimore, MD 21231
(301) 522–2668

Eposcopal Social Ministries
105 West Monument Street
Baltimore, MD 21201
(301) 837–0300

Soldier of the Cross of Christ
Evangelical International Church
724 Silver Spring Avenue
Silver Spring, MD 20910
(301) 588–8738

MASSACHUSETTS

World Relief
Emmanuel Gospel Center
2 San Juan Street
P.O. Box 18245
Boston, MA 02118
(617) 262–2265

International Institute of Boston
287 Commonwealth Avenue
Boston, MA 02115
(617) 536–1081

Catholic Diocese of Springfield
Refugee Resettlement Program
11 Pearl Street
Springfield, MA 01103
(413) 732–6365

MICHIGAN

Catholic Archdiocese of Detroit
Department of Christian Service

305 Michigan Avenue
Detroit, MI 48226
(313) 237–5900

International Institute
4138 West Vernon Avenue
Detroit, MI 48209
(313) 554–1445

Spanish Speaking Information Center
2523 Clio Road, Suite 101
Flint, MI 48504
(313) 239–4417

International Institute
11333 Joseph Campau
Hamtramck, MI 48212
(313) 365–1084
(313) 365–1092

Michigan Economic Human Development
355 East Kalamazoo
Kalamazoo, MI 49007
(616) 343–7126

Catholic Diocese of Lansing
Migration and Refugee Services
233 North Walnut Street
Lansing, MI 48933
(517) 484–1010

SER-JOBS for Progress
1535 South Warren Avenue
Saginaw, MI 48605
(517) 753–3412

MINNESOTA

Lutheran Social Services of Minnesota
Refugee Center
1730 East Superior Street
Duluth, MN 55812
(218) 728–6839

International Institute of Minnesota
1694 Como Avenue
St. Paul, MN 55108
(612) 647–0191

MISSISSIPPI

Diocese of Biloxi
Catholic Social Services
198 Reynoir Street
Biloxi, MS 39533
(601) 374–8316

MISSOURI

Guadalupe Center, Inc.
2641 Belleview
Kansas City, MO 64108
(816) 561–6885

International Institute of St. Louis
3800 Park Avenue
St. Louis, MO 63110
(314) 773–9090

MONTANA

Rural Employment Opportunities, Inc.
1143 First Avenue North, Suite 217
Billings, MT 59101
(406) 248–8280
(406) 256–1140

NEBRASKA

Nebraska Asssociation of Farmworkers, Inc.
200 South Silber
P.O. Box 1459
North Platte, NE 69103–1459
(308) 534–2630

SER-JOBS for Progress, Inc.
5002 South 33rd Street
Omaha, NE 68107-2594
(402) 734–1321

NEVADA

Catholic Social Services
1501 Las Vegas Boulevard, North
Las Vegas, NV 89101
(702) 383–8387

Catholic Community Services
Migration/Refugee Assistance and Legalization Services
190 Mill Street, Suite 3
Reno, NV 89501
(702) 323–9005

NEW HAMPSHIRE

Episcopal Legalization Center
60 Walnut Avenue
North Hampton, NH 03862
(603) 964–6671

NEW JERSEY

Catholic Social Services
Migration and Refugee Services
3098 Pleasant
Camden, NJ 08105
(609) 541–1145
(609) 541–1148

Red Cross of Eastern Union County
203 West Jersey Street
Elizabeth, NJ 07202
(201) 353–2500

International Institute of New Jersey
880 Bergen Avenue
Jersey City, NJ 07306
(201) 653–3888

National Council for the Church and Social Action, Inc.
124 North 7th Street
Newark, NJ 07102
(201) 434–5301

Lutheran Social Services
Roman Catholic Immigration Program
189 South Broad Street
P.O. Box 30
Trenton, NJ 08601-0036
(609) 393–3440

North Hudson Community Action Agency
507 26th Street
Union City, NJ 07087
(201) 866–2255

NEW MEXICO

Catholic Social Services
Archdiocese of Santa Fe
801 Mountain Road, NE
P.O. Box 25405
Albuquerque, NM 87125
(505) 247–9521

SER-JOBS for Progress
575 Alameda
Las Cruces, NM 88004
(505) 524–1946

Roswell Immigration Service Center
213 East Albuquerque
P.O. Box 2663
Roswell, NM 88201
(505) 622–1774

NEW YORK

International Center of the Capital Region
West Mall Office Plaza
875 Central Avenue
Albany, NY 12206
(518) 459–8812

Congress of Racial Equality
12-06 36th Avenue
Astoria, NY 11106
(718) 361–7437

America's Grateful Immigrants
1582 Jerome Avenue
Bronx, NY 10457
(212) 901–0059

World Relief
Joy Fellowship Church
66 East Mt. Eden Avenue
Bronx, NY 10452
(212) 583–9300

Southside Community Mission
280 Marcy Avenue
Brooklyn, NY 11211
(718) 387–3803

Catholic Migration Services, Inc.
75 Greene Avenue
P.O. Box "C"
Brooklyn, NY 11202
(718) 638–5500

International Institute of Buffalo
864 Delaware Avenue
Buffalo, NY 14209
(716) 883–1900

World Relief
First Baptist Church
42-15 Union Street
Flushing, NY 11355
(718) 538–1863

Congress of Racial Equality
412 Old Country Road
Garden City, NY 11530
(516) 741–5959

Multi-Cultural Immigration Center, Inc.
689 Columbus Avenue, Suite 8-C
New York, NY 10025
(718) 492–2459
(212) 663–0753

Movimento de Orientation al Emigrante, Inc.
557 West 156th Street
P.O. Box 430, Inwood Station
New York, NY 10034
(212) 283–1166
(212) 283–1179

International Immigrants Foundation
130 West 42nd Street, 17th Floor
New York, NY 10036
(212) 221–7255

Catholic Archdiocese of New York
Office For Legalization Services
185 Avenue D
New York, NY 10009
(212) 460–8377

International Ladies Garment Workers Union
Immigration Project
275 7th Avenue
New York, NY 10001
(212) 627–0600

Rural Opportunities, Inc.
346 Broadway
Newburgh, NY 12550
(914) 562–7350

Catholic Charities
716 Caroline Street

P.O. Box 296
Ogdensburgh, NY 13669
(315) 393–2660

Catholic Family Center
50 Chestnut Street, 5th Floor
Rochester, NY 14604
(716) 546–7220

Americanization League of
Syracuse and Onondaga
County
725 Harrison Street, Room 209
Syracuse, NY 13210
(315) 425–4120

Westchester Hispanic Coalition,
Inc.
200 Mamaroneck Avenue
White Plains, NY 10601
(914) 948–8466

NORTH CAROLINA

Catholic Social Services
1524 East Morehead Street
Charlotte, NC 28207
(704) 331–1720

Episcopal Migrant Ministry
P.O. Box 1514
Route 6 State Road 1636
Dunn, NC 28334
(919) 567–6917

OHIO

Ohio Farmworker Opportunities
Division of Rural Opportunities,
Inc.
1616 East Wooster, Suite 9
P.O. Box 186
Bowling Green, OH 43402
(419) 354–3548

Travelers Aid/International
Institute
632 Vine Street, Suite 505
Cincinnati, OH 45202
(513) 721–7660

Nationalities Services Center
1715 Euclid Avenue
Cleveland, OH 44115
(216) 781–4560

International Institute
2040 Scottwood Avenue
Toledo, OH 43620
(419) 241–9178

OKLAHOMA

Associated Catholic Charities
Immigration Services
425 NW 7th Street
P.O. Box 1516
Oklahoma City, OK 73101
(405) 232–9801

Catholic Diocese of Tulsa
Migration and Refugee Services
739 North Denver
Tulsa, OK 74106
(918) 585–8167

OREGON

OHDC-Migrant
Sunnyside Mall, Highway 395
Hermiston, OR 97838
(503) 567–5800

Immigrants Project
All Saint's Church
372 N.E. Lincoln Street
Hillsboro, OR 97124
(503) 648–4518

Treasure Valley Immigration
Counseling Service

772 North Oregon
Ontario, OR 97914
(503) 889–3121

San Salvador Vicarriate
Immigration Counseling Service
621 S.W. Morrison, Suite 205
Portland, OR 97205
(503) 221–1689

PENNSYLVANIA

Pennsylvania Farmworker Opportunities Division of Rural Opportunities, Inc.
310 Lortz Avenue
Chambersburg, PA 17201
(717) 264–2839

International Institute
330 Holland Street
P.O. Box 496
Erie, PA 16512
(814) 452–3935

Nationalities Service Center
10 South Prince Street
Lancaster, PA 17603
(717) 291–4454

Philadelphia Refugee Service Center
4047-49 Sansom Street
Philadelphia, PA 19104
(215) 386–1298

Catholic Social Service Agency
138 North 9th Street
Reading, PA 19601
(215) 374–4891

PUERTO RICO

Movimiento de Orientacion al Emigrante, Inc.
Ave Ponce de Leon 1612
Portada 23, Idif Avianca 7th Piso
Santurce, PR 00907
(809) 724–5240

RHODE ISLAND

International Institute of Rhode Island, Inc.
421 Elmwood Avenue
Providence, RI 02907
(401) 461–5940

SOUTH CAROLINA

Telamon Corporation
1804 C Savannah Highway
Charleston, SC 29407
(803) 766–1545

SOUTH DAKOTA

Lutheran Social Services
601 West 11th Street
Sioux Falls, SD 57104
(605) 336–9136

TENNESSEE

Templo Bautista
1000 South Cooper Street
Memphis, TN 38104
(901) 274–1366

Catholic Charities
Refugee Resettlement
30 White Bridge Road
Nashville, TN 37205
(615) 352–3052

TEXAS

Austin Travis County Refugee Services
1607 West 6th Street

Austin, TX 78703
(512) 478–5535

Cristo Vive for Immigrants
7524 North Lamar, Suite 106–10
Austin, TX 78752
(512) 453–8483

Catholic Diocese of Austin
Immigration Legalization Service
500 Buchanan, Suite B
P.O. Box 763
Burnet, TX 78611
(512) 756–7760

Northcutt Immigration Assistance Center
Mary King Memorial UMC
2602 Kings Road
Dallas, TX 75219
(214) 528–5827

Catholic Counseling Services
Migration and Refugee Services
3845 Oak Lawn Avenue
Dallas, TX 75219
(214) 528–8120

Catholic Diocese of El Paso
Migration and Refugee Services
1200 North Mesa
El Paso, TX 79902
(915) 532–3975

World Relief
4567 James Avenue, Suite B
Fort Worth, TX 76115
(817) 924–0748

Refugee Service Alliance
2808 Caroline Street
Houston, TX 77004
(713) 655–1720

Immigration Counseling Center
945 Lathrop
Houston, TX 77020
(713) 924–6045

San Antonio Literacy Council
1101 West Woodlawn
San Antonio, Tx 78211
(512) 732–9711

Catholic Services for Immigrants
2903 West Salinas
San Antonio, TX 78207
(512) 432–6091

Immigration Services Consultant
602 East Sixth Street, Suite 1
Weslaco, TX 78596
(512) 968–8484

UTAH

Weber Council of Spanish Speaking Organizations
369 Healy Street
Ogden, UT 84401
(801) 621–1991

Catholic Community Services
Utah Immigration Project-Outreach Program
840 Sunset Drive
Richfield, UT 84701
(801) 896–3567

Catholic Community Services of Utah
333 East South Temple, #701
Salt Lake City, UT 84111
(801) 328–9100

VERMONT

Vermont Refugee Resettlement Program
59-63 Pearl Street
Burlington, VT 05401
(802) 658–1120

VIRGINIA

Spanish Speaking Committee of Virginia
2049 North 15th Street, Suite 209
Arlington, VA 22201
(703) 558–2128

Telamon Corporation
3608 Campbell Avenue
Lynchburg, VA 24501
(804) 846–4100

Frederick Episcopal Parish Legalization Center
134 West Boscawen Street
Winchester, VA 22601
(703) 662–5843

WASHINGTON

Centro Campesino Immigrant Project
P.O. Box 800
120 Sunnyside Avenue
Granger, WA 98932
(509) 854–2222

Washington State Migrant Council
Mabton MHS
North 1st & B Streets
P.O. Box 128
Mabton, WA 98935
(509) 894–4322

Washington State Migrant Council
Moses Lake MHS
5th and Chestnut Streets
Moses Lake, WA 98837
(509) 765–6724

Washington State Migrant Council
Mt. Vernon MHS
2010 North LaVenture
Mt. Vernon, WA 98273
(206) 428–3993

Washington Association of Churches
3902 South Ferdinand
Seattle, WA 98118
(206) 721–5288

Hispanic Immigration Program
Catholic Archdiocese of Seattle
3600 South Graham
Seattle, WA 98118
(206) 721–4752

Catholic Family Services
West 1104 Heroy
Spokane, WA 99205
(509) 456–7153

Enterprise for Progress in the Community
1910 Englewood Avenue
Yakima, WA 98902
(509) 248–3950

WEST VIRGINIA

Catholic Diocese of Wheeling-Charleston
Migration and Refugee Services
901 Quarrier Street, Room 201
Charleston, WV 25301
(304) 343–1036

WISCONSIN

Spanish Centers of Racine
Kenosha and Walroth, Inc.
1212 57th Street
Kenosha, WI
(414) 552–7830

The Council for the Spanish Speaking

614 West National Avenue
Milwaukee, WI 53204
(414) 384–3700

La Casa de Esperanza
410 Arcadian Avenue
Waukesha, WI 53186
(414) 547–0887

WYOMING

Metropolitan Analysis and
Retrieval Systems, Inc.
Warland Municipal Airport
Terminal Building Airport Road
Warland, WY 82401
(307) 347–2483